Better Homes and Gardens®

BIG
Book of
KIDS'
CRAFTS

301 projects for kids 4 to 12

Meredith® Books
Des Moines, Iowa

BIG Book of KIDS' CRAFTS

Editor: Dan Rosenberg
Copy Chief: Terri Fredrickson
Publishing Operations Manager: Karen Schirm
Edit and Design Production Coordinator: Mary Lee Gavin
Editorial Assistant: Cheryl Eckert, Kairee Windsor
Marketing Product Managers: Aparna Pande, Isaac Petersen,
    Gina Rickert, Stephen Rogers, Brent Wiersma, Tyler Woods
Book Production Managers: Pam Kvitne, Marjorie J. Schenkelberg,
    Rick von Holdt, Mark Weaver
Contributing Copy Editor: Margaret Smith
Contributing Proofreaders: Kristin Bienert, Callie Dunbar
Technical Illustrator: Chris Neubauer Graphics, Inc.

Meredith® **Books**
Executive Director, Editorial: Gregory H. Kayko
Executive Director, Design: Matt Strelecki
Senior Editor/Group Manager: Vicki Ingham

Publisher and Editor in Chief: James D. Blume
Editorial Director: Linda Raglan Cunningham
Executive Director, Marketing: Jeffrey B. Myers
Executive Director, New Business Development: Todd M. Davis
Executive Director, Sales: Ken Zagor
Director, Operations: George A. Susral
Director, Production: Douglas M. Johnston
Business Director: Jim Leonard

Vice President and General Manager: Douglas J. Guendel

Better Homes and Gardens® **Magazine**
Editor in Chief: Karol DeWulf Nickell

Meredith Publishing Group
President: Jack Griffin
Senior Vice President: Bob Mate

Meredith Corporation
Chairman and Chief Executive Officer: William T. Kerr
President and Chief Operating Officer: Stephen M. Lacy

In Memoriam: E.T. Meredith III (1933-2003)

All of us at Meredith® Books are dedicated to providing you with
information and ideas to create beautiful and useful projects.
We welcome your comments and suggestions. Write to us at:
Meredith Books, Crafts Editorial Department, 1716 Locust Street—
LN112, Des Moines, IA 50309-3023.

If you would like to purchase any of our crafts, cooking, gardening,
home improvement, or home decorating and design books, check
wherever quality books are sold. Or visit us at: bhgbooks.com

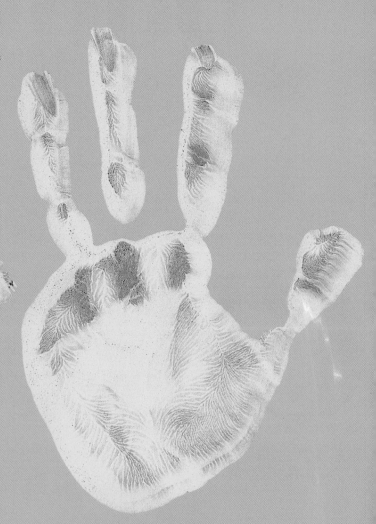

Welcome to the world of Kids' crafts—a magical world of imagination and play!

Whether this is the first book of children's crafts that you have purchased or one of many on your crafting shelf, you will be pleased with this big book of fun. You'll find projects to make with bright and colorful paint, printed and textured papers, oh-so-fun pliable clay, glittering beads, and soft and foldable fabric. You'll find dozens of projects to make outside on sunny days or ideas to keep busy indoors on cold or rainy days. There are projects for a "spooktacular" Halloween, imaginative holiday ideas galore, lacy valentines to make and give, and Easter eggs to decorate. You'll find gifts for little ones to make all by themselves and projects that you and your child will love to create together.

So enjoy the magical world of kids' crafts. We know you'll love every minute you spend crafting.

– The editors of the Big Book of Kids' Crafts

contents

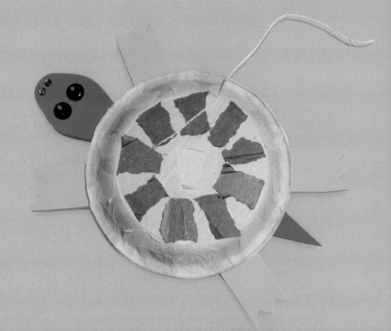

a note to parents

Welcome to a project-packed book that will jump-start your kids' creativity like never before! It's designed for children 4 to 12 years of age. This exciting book inspires young crafters to experiment with new crafts supplies, learn cool techniques, and use their imaginations to create wonderful projects that both of you will treasure while being entertained, challenged, and excited.

With hundreds of projects to make, you'll know you can refer to this book when the kids are tempted to say, "I need something to do." Your child will be guided through page after page of painting projects, paper crafts, bead making, holiday trims, and more—all accompanied by a detailed materials list, step-by-step instructions, and helpful photos. Plus there are crafting tips and suggestions that offer options and encourage kids to expand their skills.

When projects require a tool or include a step that may be a bit tricky, we mention that help is needed from a grown-up to ensure your child's crafting success and safety.

Beyond the basics, kids will learn a host of new techniques. They'll discover how to mix colors and how to make their own rubber stamp. They'll be introduced to several painting techniques. Before you know it, your child will master decoupage, jewelry making, printing, and more to fill them with a sense of accomplishment and pride.

When helping your child decide which

projects to make, look over the list of supplies. Some crafts use items that you may have around the house. Others may require a trip to the store. When supplies are unusual, we'll tell you where to find them. To encourage young crafters, it's a good idea to have some basic supplies on hand. We suggest:

* Scissors (straight and decorative-edge)
* Tracing paper
* Pencils
* Marking pens
* Thick white crafts glue
* Glue stick
* Colored paper
* Newspapers, waxed paper, or old plastic tablecloth (to protect the work surface)
* Old clothes (little Picassos get messy sometimes!)

To keep your supplies organized, specify a drawer or plastic container to store the items. When the crafting bug bites, the supplies can be quickly gathered and the fun can begin!

Have a wonderful time crafting with your child. We've made it so FUN and EASY! The only hard part? Deciding which project to do first!

create something FUN

Bookworms, puppets, and fish galore–paint all these things,
and then paint some more! You'll make pretty note cards and
cool shoelaces, plus sunshiny beach pails to take places.
Take time for a paint shirt, don't be in a rush–and remember
to grab your paint and a brush!

with paint and markers!

happy cards

You could start your own card business with these no-fail cards designed by you! To learn how to make one-of-a-kind greetings, just turn the page.

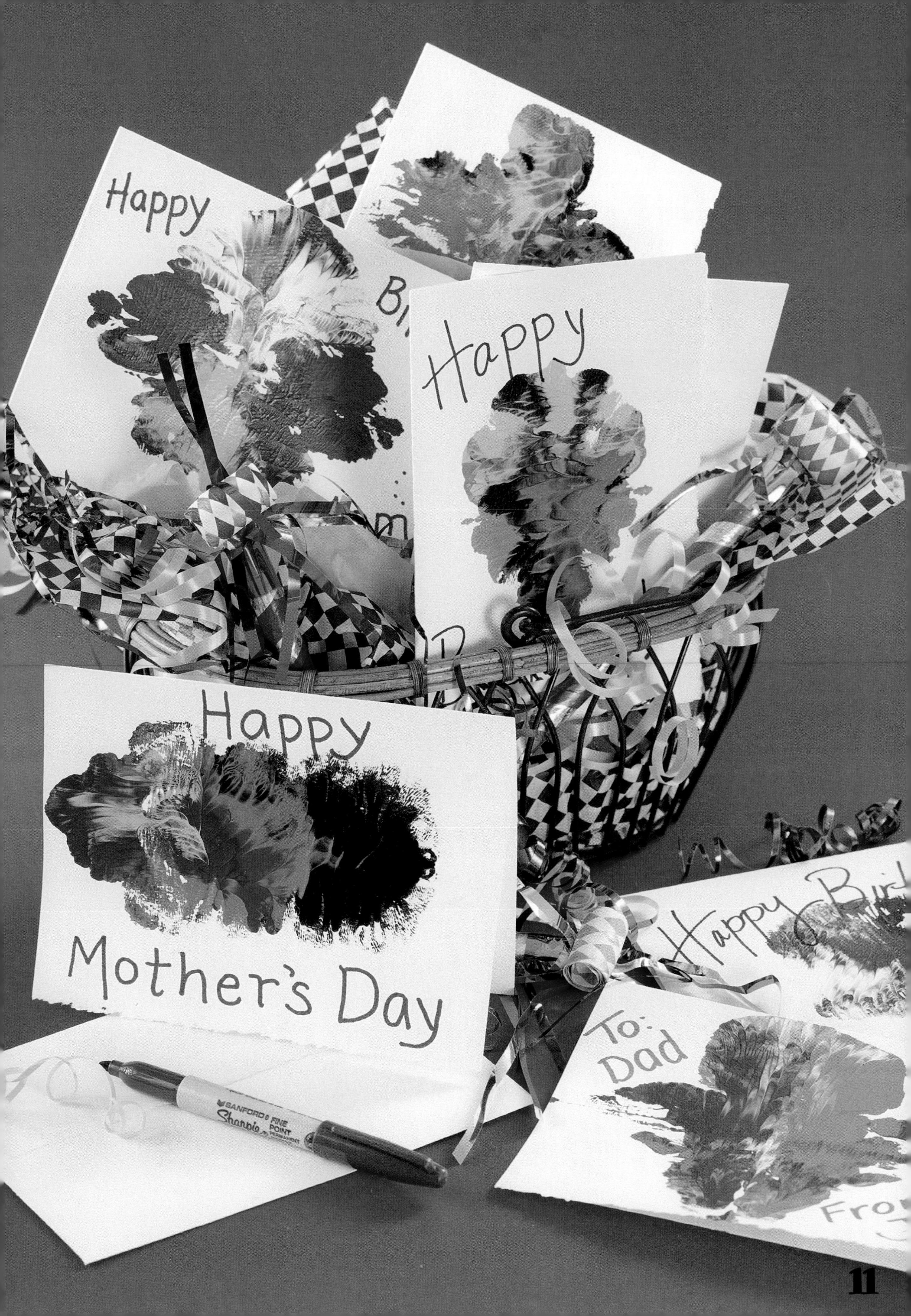
Happy
Happy
Happy
Mother's Day
To: Dad

happy cards

YOU'LL NEED

Sheet of paper
Tempera or acrylic paints
    in colors you like
Paintbrush
Purchased blank
    greeting cards
Colored marking pens

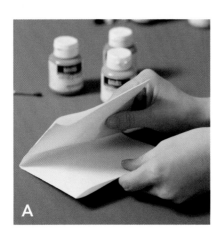

A

B

HERE'S HOW

1 Fold the piece of paper in half and crease the fold. Fold the paper in half again as shown in Photo A, *above*, bringing the folded edges together, and crease.

2 Choose three or more paint colors that blend together well. Look at the color wheel and color mixing guide, *page 13,* for help. One color at a time, dip a paintbrush in each paint and let it glob on the folds of the paper (see Photo B).

Color Wheel

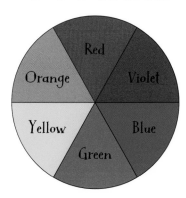

Color Mixing Guide

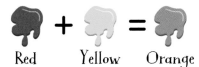

Red + Yellow = Orange

Red + Blue = Violet

Yellow + Blue = Green

Red + White = Pink

Black + White = Gray

Blue + Black = Navy Blue

Orange + Green = Brown

3 Fold the paper again and gently rub the colors together as shown in Photo C.

C

4 Open up the paper. Turn the paper upside down on the front of the blank greeting card and rub the paper gently. Pull the top paper off the card as shown in Photo D.

5 Let the paint dry. Use a marking pen to write a greeting on the front or inside of the card.

D

GOOD IDEA
Don't take too long rubbing the paint or it will begin to dry and may stick.

veggie print wraps

Are there vegetables left in your refrigerator? If you didn't eat them all for dinner—paint with them! To learn how to make colorful wrapping papers by printing with vegetables, turn the page.

veggie print wraps

YOU'LL NEED

Newspapers
Raw firm vegetables and
    fruits such as carrots,
    celery, peppers,
    artichokes, apples,
    and pears
Sharp knife
Acrylic paint in colors
    you like
Disposable plate
Plain-color wrapping
    papers, paper sacks,
    or newsprint papers

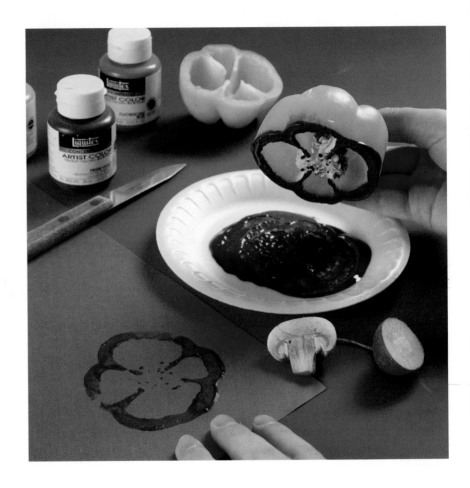

HERE'S HOW

1 Cover your work
surface with newspapers.

2 You will get a different
design depending on how
you cut the vegetables or
fruits. It is important you
cut them with a flat side
so the paint can cover
them evenly.

3 Pour some paint onto
the plate and spread it
around to make a
smooth surface.

4 Dip the cut vegetable
or fruit into the paint and
practice printing on
paper sacks, newsprint,
or newspapers. Use only a
little paint so the design
does not run together.
Wash the paint off the
vegetable before using
another color of paint.

5 Lay the wrapping
paper on the table. After
you like how your fruit or
vegetable is printing, dip
it into the paint and press
it firmly on the paper.
Repeat the design until
you like what you see!

6 Let the paint dry.
Wrap your gift in the
paper; add ribbon to
finish (see *page 17*).

GOOD IDEA

You can use stamped papers for place mats, greeting cards, and book covers too!

stick-to-it puzzle

Here is a puzzle that will stick with you. Paint an original work of art using some of our watercolor ideas, and then turn your masterpiece into a magnetic puzzle. To learn how, see the next page.

YOU'LL NEED

Watercolor paper
Scissors
Masking tape
Watercolor paints
Water in dish
Paintbrush
Pencil
Ruler
Rubber cement or
   crayons
3½×2-inch self-stick
   magnets made for
   attaching business
   cards (available at
   office supply stores
   and discount stores)
Paper towels

HERE'S HOW

1 Decide how big you want to make your puzzle. (After your puzzle is done, each piece will be the same size as one magnet.) Cut a piece of paper ½ inch larger on all sides than the finished puzzle. (We used six self-stick magnets for our puzzle.

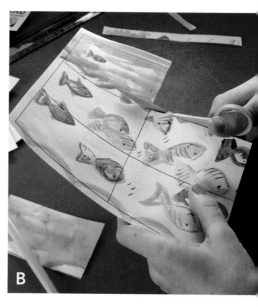

We cut the piece of paper 8×7 inches and trimmed ½ inch from all the sides where we put tape. Our finished puzzle is 7×6 inches.)

2 Tape the watercolor paper to the table or to a board. As shown in Photo A, *above,* paint your picture any way you wish. Use some of the watercolor techniques shown on *pages 20–21.*

3 Let your picture dry and remove the tape.

4 Use a pencil and ruler to mark where to cut your picture. Each piece should fit on one magnet. Cut out the pieces to make a puzzle, as shown in Photo B.

5 Peel off the backing on the magnets and attach the magnets to the back of each piece of the puzzle as shown in Photo C.

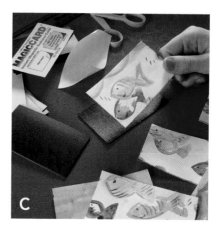

6 Put the pieces of the puzzle together and put it on the refrigerator for everyone to try!

watercolor techniques

Paint your picture any way you wish. Here are some fun watercolor techniques to try:

rubber cement resist painting

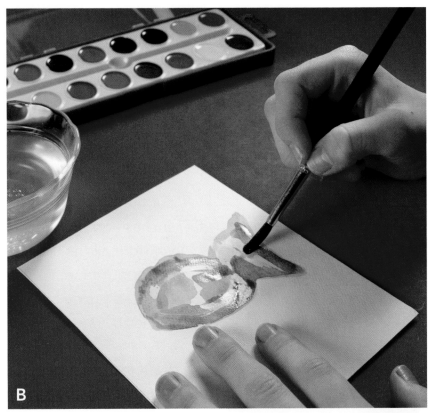

B

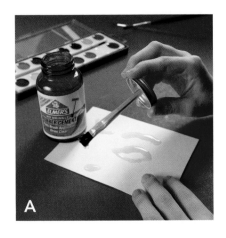

A

1 Before you start painting, drizzle some rubber cement on the paper wherever you want the paper to stay white after you paint as shown in Photo A, *above*.

2 Let the rubber cement dry. Now paint over the rubber cement as if it weren't there, as shown in Photo B. Let the watercolor paint dry completely.

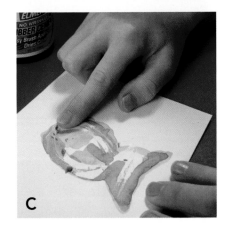

C

3 Use your finger to rub the rubber cement off the painting as shown in Photo C to leave white highlights on your picture.

D

F

crayon resist painting

1 Before you paint, draw some of your picture with crayon (see Photo D).

E

2 Paint directly over the crayon as shown in Photo E. The crayon will show through the paint and make an interesting picture.

wet on wet

1 Paint part of your picture using clear water. Use your paintbrush to drop in the colors you wish as shown in Photo F. The paint will run into the water on the paper and make a soft look.

GOOD IDEA
Sprinkle salt over a watercolor painting to look like tiny snowflakes.

G

dry brush

1 Use this technique when you want to put details in your picture. Paint your picture as you wish. When the picture is almost dry, paint details as shown in Photo G. Your brush should be damp but not wet. Dry it off with a paper towel if it is too wet. Use thick watercolor paint and move the brush quickly to brush on details.

rainbow bookworm

It's always fun to have a friend to read with—and this painted and spectacled bookworm is waiting to read with you! Make him with plastic foam balls and lots of colorful paint.

A

YOU'LL NEED

Table knife

Eleven 2-inch plastic foam balls (seven for the bookworm and four to help hold the balls while painting)

Seven round toothpicks

Acrylic paint in turquoise, purple, bright pink, yellow, green, red, and orange

Flat paintbrush

Pipe cleaners, three of each paint color used for the body, plus one additional yellow

Thick white crafts glue

Two 18-mm wiggle eyes

⅓-inch orange pom-pom

Scissors

8-inch piece of medium crafts wire

HERE'S HOW

1 Use a table knife to cut four of the plastic foam balls in half. Place them on your work surface flat side down.

GOOD IDEA

Be sure to wash your paintbrush with soap and water before changing colors.

2 Push one end of a toothpick into the center of one plastic foam ball. Stick the other end into one of the cut balls as shown in Photo A, *above*, to make it easy to paint the ball and keep it still for drying. Do the same with all of the other whole balls, painting each ball a different color. Let the paint dry (this may take an hour or so) and remove the toothpicks.

(continued on page 24)

rainbow bookworm

3 To make the bookworm antennae, fold one yellow pipe cleaner in half and twist the ends into spirals.

4 Insert the folded part of the antennae in the top of the ball for the head. Glue the eyes and the pom-pom nose to the face, looking at the photograph on *page 22* to help you.

B

GOOD IDEA
Use this method to make other creatures, such as dragonflies, dinosaurs, and ants.

5 Cut the rest of the pipe cleaners in half. Fold each piece in half, twist the ends together, and fold the pieces into "Z" shapes to make feet. Match pipe cleaner colors to the painted plastic foam balls and insert the ends of the pipe cleaner feet into the balls, using Photo B, and the photo on *page 22* as guides.

C

6 Put a dot of glue on one end of a toothpick and push it into one of the painted balls as shown in Photo C to connect the balls. Push the other end into a second ball. Put all seven balls together in the same way. Let the glue dry.

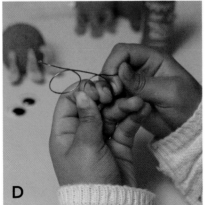

D

7 Use craft wire to make a circle the size of a nickel about 2 inches from one end of the wire. Make a second circle next to the first, as shown in Photo D. Bend the ends to make bows for the glasses. Put the glasses on the head and push the wire ends into the back.

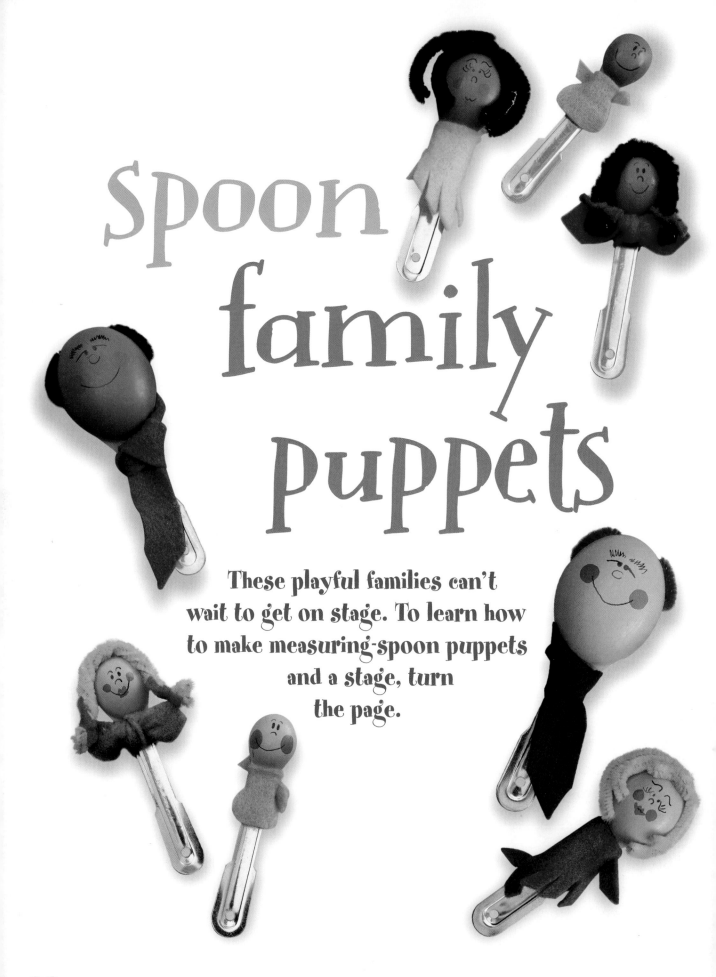

Spoon family puppets

These playful families can't wait to get on stage. To learn how to make measuring-spoon puppets and a stage, turn the page.

spoon family puppets

YOU'LL NEED

1 set of metal measuring
    spoons
Opaque marking pen
    in skin color and pink
Permanent fine-line black
    marking pen
Pencil
Tracing paper
Scissors
Felt scraps
Thick white crafts glue
Pipe cleaners in yellow
    and brown or black

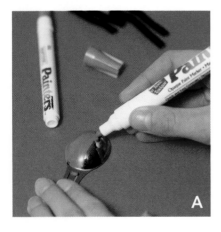

HERE'S HOW

1 Color the back of the spoons using skin color opaque marking pen as shown in Photo A, *left.* Let it dry and color on a second coat. Let dry.

2 Use the patterns on *page 30* and a permanent black marking pen to draw faces on each spoon as shown in Photo B.

3 Use a pencil and tracing paper to trace the clothing patterns. Cut out the patterns.

4 Draw around the pattern pieces on felt scraps, using whatever colors of felt you like. Cut out the felt clothing around the traced markings.

5 Tie the felt bib onto the baby and use a drop of crafts glue to hold it in place. Let the glue dry.

6 Tie the scarf onto the big sister spoon and put a drop of glue under the felt to hold it in place. Let the glue dry.

7 Tie the scarf onto the mom (see Photo C) and put a drop of glue under the felt to hold it in place. Let the glue dry.

8 Tie the necktie onto the dad and put a drop of glue under the felt to hold it in place. Let the glue dry.

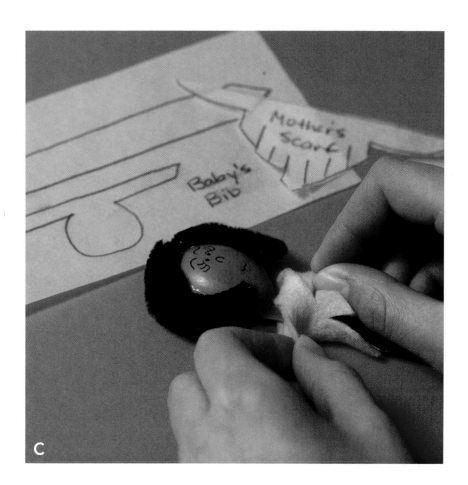

C

9 Choose a pipe cleaner color for the big sister's hair. Cut the pipe cleaner into three equal pieces. Twist the pieces together and shape them to the top of the spoon. Tie small scraps of felt at each end for bows. Glue the hair to the top of the head.

(continued on page 30)

GOOD IDEA

Use tiny ribbons, jewels, buttons, or marking pens to decorate the clothes.

29

spoon family puppets

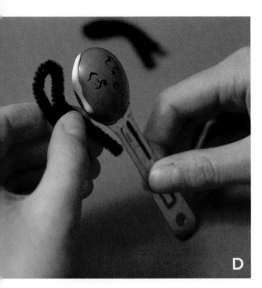

D

10 Choose a pipe cleaner color for the mom's hair. Cut one pipe cleaner 3 inches long and one pipe cleaner 4 inches long. Fold the pieces in half. On the 4-inch piece, fold the loop end over to make bangs. Glue the hair pieces to each side of the head as shown in Photo D.

11 Choose a pipe cleaner color for dad's hair. Cut two 1-inch-long pieces. Bend the ends and glue one piece of hair to each side of the head.

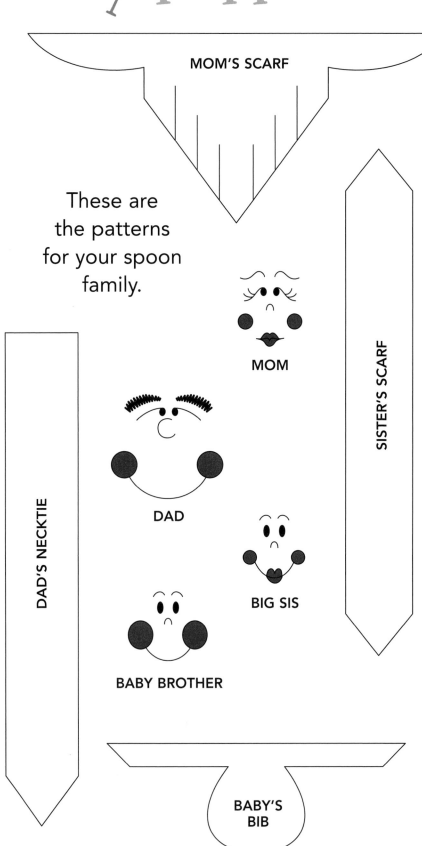

MOM'S SCARF

These are the patterns for your spoon family.

MOM

SISTER'S SCARF

DAD

DAD'S NECKTIE

BIG SIS

BABY BROTHER

BABY'S BIB

puppet stage

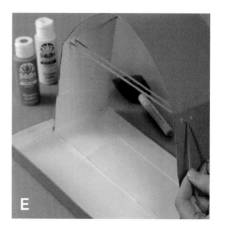

E

YOU'LL NEED

Shoe box with lid
Scissors
Paper punch
Thick white crafts glue
Acrylic paint in two colors
Paintbrush
36-inches of yarn
Paper napkins or
    two 6×6-inch scraps
    of fabric; paper clips
Photograph stickers
    or gems

HERE'S HOW

1 Ask a grown-up to help you cut out the bottom of a shoe box.

2 Use the illustration, *below right,* to punch two holes at the top of the short ends of the shoe box (about an inch apart and opposite each other).

3 Cut off one long side of the shoebox lid. Lay the lid with the sides pointing up.

4 Spread glue on the outside of the long side of the shoe box that is farthest away from the punched holes. With the glue side down, press the shoe box to the lid, lining up the cut edge of the lid with the uncut edge of the box (see photo E). Let the glue dry.

5 Use whatever color of paint you like to paint the inside and floor of the stage. Apply as many coats as needed to cover any writing on your shoe box. (Be sure to let the paint dry between coats!)

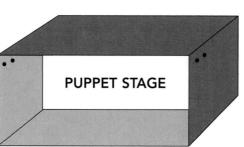

PUPPET STAGE

6 Paint the outside of the stage using a different color of paint. Paint on more than one coat if you need to cover up the markings on the shoe box. Let the paint dry.

7 Thread the yarn through the punched holes as shown in Photo E. Pull the yarn carefully so the top of the stage curves. Tie the ends of the yarn in a knot.

8 To make a curtain for the stage, fold the napkin or fabric scraps like a fan and use paper clips to hang them from the yarn.

9 Decorate the outside of the stage however you like, using funny photograph stickers, gems, more paint— whatever you think is fun!

31

Keep your fish company with one or more of these brilliantly colored fish clings. If you don't have fish, attach your clings to a window or mirror!

rainbow-fish
clings

YOU'LL NEED

White paper; pencil
DecoArt reusable
   Styrene Blank sheet
DecoArt Black Leading
DecoArt Liquid Rainbow
   paint in fuschia, lemon,
   lime, orange, lollipop,
   red, yellow, raindrop,
   and turquoise
Toothpicks

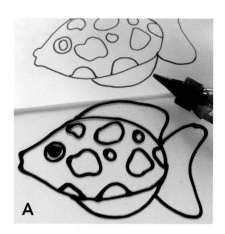

A

HERE'S HOW

1 Trace the fish pattern, *page 35*, onto white paper or make a copy on a photocopier. Add decorative outlines for inside shapes if you wish. Peel the protective plastic off the Styrene Blank sheet. Lay the tracing right side up on your work surface. Place the

sheet over the tracing. Retrace the solid lines of the fish body on the sheet with the black leading, as shown in Photo A, *left*. Hold the leading bottle in your hand like a pencil and just above the sheet. Squeeze the bottle gently with even pressure.

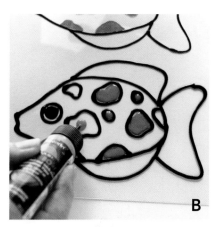

B

2 Look at the photographs on *pages 32* and *34* and draw leaded dots or lines inside the outlines as shown in Photo B. Let dry for 2 hours.

3 Fill in the leaded areas with the paints. Use the tip of a toothpick to swirl colors together that are side by side. Fill in the whole leaded area so the paint touches the leading as shown in Photo C.

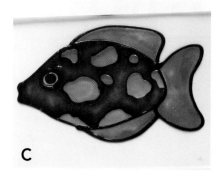

C

4 Let the paint dry for 24 hours or until it is see-through. Carefully peel the fish cling off the sheet.

5 Press the fish onto a hard surface, such as a fish tank, window, mirror, plastic container, or candle. Do not press it on a wall because the paint might come off on the wall.

GOOD IDEA
When you aren't using your fish cling, put it on a blank Styrene sheet.

rainbow-fish clings

Use these fish for
ideas on how to paint
your rainbow-fish clings.

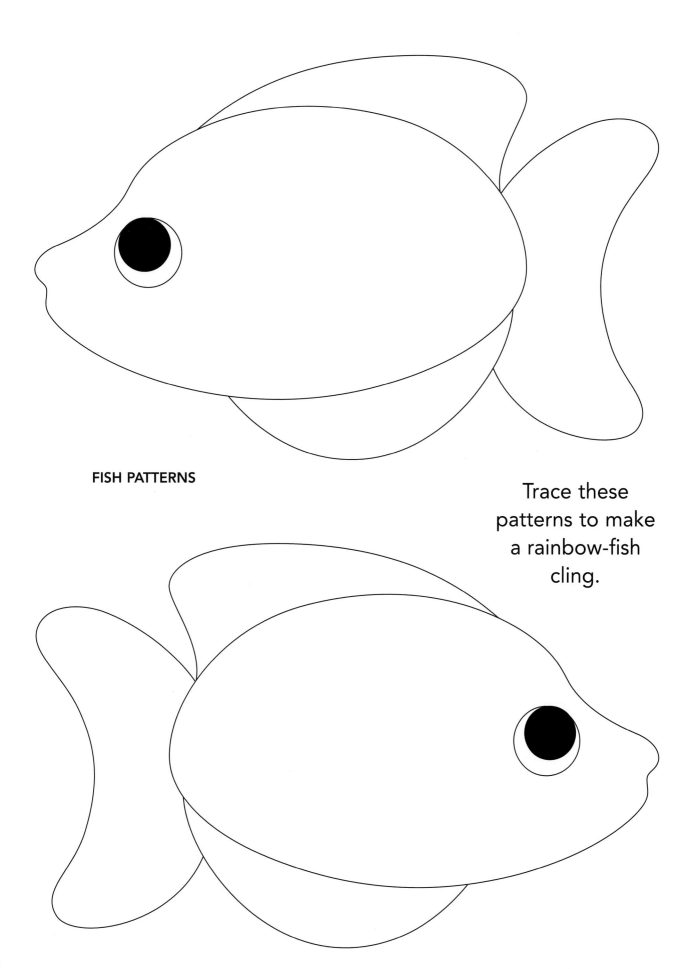

FISH PATTERNS

Trace these patterns to make a rainbow-fish cling.

Make a bowl for your pup
by painting on bright
designs and a special name.

Puppy bowl

YOU'LL NEED

Dog food bowl
Acrylic enamel paint in
   colors you like
Paintbrush

GOOD IDEA
Use sticker
letters or designs
on a dish for
your kitty or
puppy.

HERE'S HOW

1 Wash the dog food bowl. Let it dry. Do not touch the areas to be painted.

2 Paint your dog's name on the bowl as you wish. You can tilt some of the letters as shown, *opposite*. Paint lines above or below the letters and paint stripes around the bottom edge of the bowl.

3 Paint squiggles, zigzags, or any other shapes around the bowl. Make dots by dipping a paintbrush handle in paint and dotting on the surface. Let the paint dry.

earring tree

A blast to make, wear,
and put away—earrings have
never been so much fun!

YOU'LL NEED

For the earrings
Thick white crafts glue
Buttons, paper clips,
    small appliqués, beads,
    wiggle eyes
Earring backs
    Acrylic paint
        White cardboard
        or disposable
        plastic plate
        Pencil with
        round-tip eraser
        Small ceramic
        tiles
        Eraser topper in
        square shape
For the earring holder
Picture frame
Plastic canvas in any color
Pencil
    Scissors
        Thick white crafts glue

HERE'S HOW

A

For the earrings

1 Glue buttons, paper clips, appliqués, beads, or wiggle eyes to the earring backs as shown in Photo A, *above*. Let the glue dry.

B

2 For the tile earrings, put paint on a scrap of white cardboard or on a plastic plate. Dip the

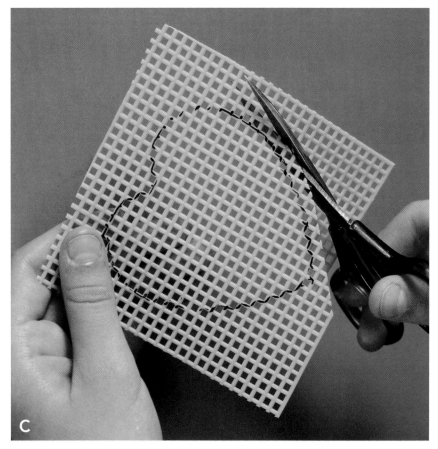

C

round eraser end of a pencil in the paint and dab it onto the tile for a flower center. Dip the square top eraser into the paint to make petals as shown in Photo B. Let the paint dry. Glue an earring back to the tile. Let the glue dry.

For the earring holder

1 Ask a grown-up to help you take the glass out of the picture frame. Lay the frame on the plastic canvas and draw around the inside of the frame. Use scissors to cut around the shape, leaving about ¼ inch all the way around the shape as shown in Photo C.

2 Use crafts glue to glue the plastic canvas in the back of the frame. Let the glue dry.

3 Insert the pierced earring posts through the plastic canvas and attach the earring backs to hold the earrings in place.

39

Snazzy yo-yos

You'll be the talk of the neighborhood with your own decorated yo-yo to show your stuff.

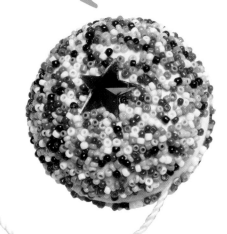

YOU'LL NEED

Waxed paper
Old or new yo-yo
Acrylic paint in colors you like
Paintbrushes
Thick white crafts glue
Beads, jewels, or flower shapes cut from lace pieces

HERE'S HOW

1 Cover your work surface with waxed paper. Paint one side of the yo-yo. (You don't need to paint the inside by the string.) Let the paint dry.

2 Turn the yo-yo over and paint the other side. Let that side dry. Give each side another coat of paint. Let both sides dry very well.

3 To paint dots on the yo-yo, dip the paintbrush handle in paint and dot it onto the yo-yo as shown in the photo *above*.

4 Glue beads, jewels, or shapes cut from lace pieces onto your yo-yo.

GOOD IDEA
If you don't like how the painting is turning out, wipe it off while it's wet and start over!

best friends
picture frame

Make some new miniature friends!
They look adorable perched on a plain picture
frame that shows off your life-size pals.

YOU'LL NEED
FOR ONE DOLL

Pencil
Round top clothespin
Acrylic paints
Black fine-tip
    permanent
    marking pen
Two ⅛-inch wooden
    dowel
Thick white crafts
    glue
5×7-inch acrylic flat
    frameless frame

HERE'S HOW

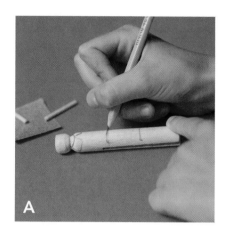

A

1 Use the photograph, *opposite*, and the patterns, *right*, to draw hair and clothes on the clothespin with a pencil as shown in Photo A, *above*.

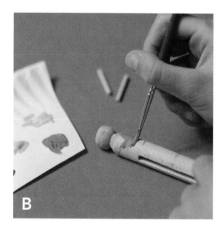

B

2 Paint the clothes and hair in colors you like (see Photo B).

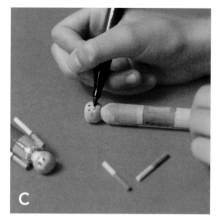

C

3 Use the black marker to draw a face as shown in Photo C, using one of the face patterns for ideas. Use the marker to draw legs and other details.

4 Paint the top of the arm dowels for sleeves and let dry. Glue the dowels toward the front of the slit in the clothespin on each side of the clothespin.

5 Put your favorite picture in the acrylic frame. Put the frame together. Clip several clothespin friends at the top.

Here are some ideas to help you decorate your clothespins.

43

lively laces

Your shoes will be adorable all laced up
with shoelaces designed by you!

YOU'LL NEED

Waxed paper or a
   grocery bag
White flat shoelaces for
   athletic shoes
Permanent marking pens
   in colors you like

HERE'S HOW

1 Cover your work table
with waxed paper or a
grocery bag before you
start to color. Just in case
your marking pen slips,
you won't get marker on
the table.

2 If the shoelace is
hard to color because
it moves around too
much, tape the lace ends
to your work surface.

3 Use permanent
marking pens to decorate
one side of each shoelace
with a bright pattern or
stripes as shown in Photo
A, *above*. Let the marker
dry. Decorate the other
side of the lace.

GOOD IDEA
Color only on the
shoelaces. If you color
the plastic ends, the
color will rub off
and be messy.

fish

Give your smallest pet company by painting a school of little swimmers on a glass fishbowl.

bowls

Fishbowl
Glass paints in
 colors you like
Paper plate
Paintbrush
Colored rubber bands

HERE'S HOW

1 Wash the fishbowl. Let it dry. Do no touch the areas to be painted.

2 Place a small amount of paint to be used for the fish bodies on the plate. Dip your finger in the paint. Press your finger on the fishbowl. Make more paint fingerprints until you have about 12 fish bodies on the bowl. Let the paint dry.

3 Use other colors of paints to add details to the fish as shown, *opposite* and *above*. Let the paint dry.

4 Put three rubber bands around the rim of the bowl. Group a few rubber bands together and tie a rubber band around the middle to make a bow. Tie another rubber band around the middle and through the rubber bands on the rim.

GOOD IDEA
Make fingerprint flowers on a rose bowl by making a center and five or six petals around it.

47

Sunshine Sandals

Have fun in the sun with these brightly painted summer sandals!

Vinyl sandals
Acrylic enamel paints in purple, pink, white, orange, and lime green
Dimensional fabric paint in lime green, optional
Paintbrush
Comb
Rag

HERE'S HOW

1 Your sandals can be smooth or can have grooves and stripes in them like these. Wash and dry the sandals before painting.

2 Paint the entire top of each sandal purple. Let the paint dry.

3 Paint stripes of pink and orange or other colors that you like. Let the paint dry.

4 Paint checks or dots over the solid colors. To make dots, dip the paintbrush handle in paint and dot it onto the surface.

5 To make stripes with tiny vertical lines, first paint the pink color. Let it dry (this is important so the paint doesn't scratch off). Paint green over the pink. While the paint is wet, use a comb to drag over the wet green paint to take away some green and leave the pink lines showing through. Wipe the paint off the comb between each pass of the comb. You also can use fabric paint for the top layer to comb off, which works well for making a thicker texture.

stick people glassware

Create playful glassware for your family using your own artistic designs.

YOU'LL NEED

Paper; pencil
Stick people art
Plain glass cake stand
Plain, clear drinking
    glasses
Masking tape
Many colors of gloss
    glass paint, such as
    Deco Art
Paintbrush

HERE'S HOW

1 Draw stick figures on paper. Place the drawing inside the glass or cake dome and tape it down.

2 Read the instructions on the paint bottle. Trace the stick figures with paint on the outside of the glass. Let the paint

dry. Remove the pattern taped inside. Paint the stem of the cake plate if you wish. Let the paint dry.

3 Ask a grown-up for help to bake the painted glassware in the oven if the paint instructions say to bake it. Let the glassware cool.

laundry bag

Keep your clothes off the floor with this cheerful laundry bag that bursts with fun people.

YOU'LL NEED

Fabric laundry bag in a
  bright color
Cardboard piece smaller
  than the laundry bag
Fabric paint pens in black
  and colors you like
Embroidery floss
Needle
Scissors

HERE'S HOW

1 Slip the cardboard inside the laundry bag so the paint does not go through to the other side. Use the photograph of the bag, *opposite*, for ideas. Draw boys and girls or other designs on one side of the laundry bag with a black paint pen. Let the paint dry.

2 Use colored paint pens to make clothes, shoes, and faces as you wish. Let the paint dry.

3 Ask a grown-up to help you thread embroidery floss through a needle. Make a stitch through the fabric where you want to make bows. Tie floss into bows and trim the ends. To make bows between the drawings, make stitches through the bag with floss and knot the floss on the right side. Trim the ends of the floss.

fancy flowerpots

These fun-to-make clay pots are the perfect gift for just about anyone and are great for holding favorite things.

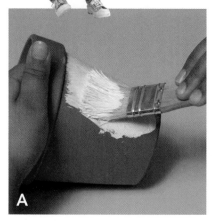

A

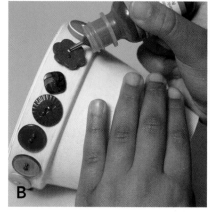

B

C

YOU'LL NEED

Medium flat paintbrush
Acrylic paint in white and green
4-inch clay pot
Assorted buttons
Thick white crafts glue
Paint pens in colors you like
Medium round artist's paintbrush

HERE'S HOW

1 Use the flat brush to paint the outside of the clay pot white, as shown in Photo A. Let the paint dry.

2 Glue whatever colorful buttons you like around the top of the painted clay pot, leaving a small space between each of the buttons as shown in Photo B. Let the glue dry.

Use paint pens in colors you choose to put dots of paint over the holes in the buttons.

3 Use the round brush to paint green stems and leaves below each button, as shown in Photo C, if you wish.

GOOD IDEA
Lay a button on each side of the flowerpot to keep it from rolling when you paint.

flowery umbrella

YOU'LL NEED

Flat, expandable sponges (available at crafts stores)
Permanent black marking pen
Flower-shape cookie cutters, optional
Scissors; dish of water
Newspapers
Fabric paint pens in green and colors you like
Umbrella

HERE'S HOW

1 Use a marking pen to draw stem, leaf, and simple tulip, daffodil, and daisy shapes on flat sponges. If you like, trace flower-shape cookie cutters for the designs. Cut out the sponge shapes. Soak sponges in water to expand them; wring out the sponges.

2 Cover the work surface with newspapers.

Squeeze green paint onto the stem sponge piece. Spread the paint evenly across the pattern using a scrap of sponge. Open the umbrella. Hold the stem sponge by its sides and press it on the fabric as shown in the photo, *right.* Hold your other hand underneath the umbrella to hold it steady.

3 Put green paint on the leaf-shape sponge and press it on the umbrella. Add flowers using favorite colors of paint. Let the paint dry.

GOOD IDEA
Buy alphabet stamps to write "Rain, Rain, Go Away" on your umbrella.

Write your best friend a note on this frog-stamped stationery!

ribbit
note cards

YOU'LL NEED

Tracing paper
Pen or pencil; scissors
Foam shoe innersoles
Small pieces of
    scrap wood
Thick white crafts glue
Green ink pad
Yellow cardstock
Red and blue puffy paint
Wiggle eyes in small
    and medium

HERE'S HOW

1 Trace the frog patterns, *opposite*, onto paper. Cut out the patterns. Draw around the patterns on the foam innersoles as shown in Photo A. Cut out the frog shapes.

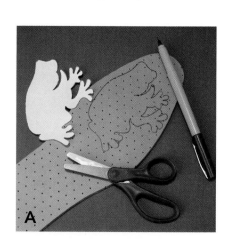

A

3 Press the frog design onto the ink pad. Press the inked stamp onto cardstock. Carefully lift the stamp from the paper so the ink does not smudge as shown in Photo B. Use paint to add a tongue, fly, or other details. Glue a small and medium eye to each frog.

2 Glue the frogs to a scrap of wood. Let the glue dry.

FROG PATTERNS

Trace these leaping frog patterns. When you print them, they'll be backwards!

painted
mosaic
frame

Make a neon-bright frame of painted wooden
tiles for Grandma—and remember your photo!

YOU'LL NEED

Waxed paper or a paper
   grocery bag
Masking tape; ruler
Forty 1-inch-square
   wooden pieces
1 inch flat sponge brush
Acrylic paint in white
   and black
Fluorescent paints in
   colors you like
Paper towels
Container with water
Gloss varnish
7-inch-square papier-
   mâché frame with a
   3-inch-square opening
   (available at crafts
   stores); photo
Thick white crafts glue

HERE'S HOW

1 Cover your work
surface with waxed paper
or a grocery bag. Tear off
five 12 inch strips of
masking tape. Place the
strips sticky side up on
your work surface. Use
small pieces of tape to
tape down the ends of
the strips. Press eight
wooden squares onto
each tape strip.

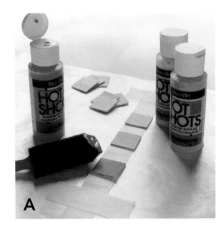

A

2 Use the 1 inch flat
brush to paint all the
wooden squares white.
Let the paint dry.

3 Paint all the wooden
squares with the
fluorescent paint as
shown in Photo A, *above*,
using the colors in the
photograph, *opposite*,
as a guide or using a
combination of your
choice. Let the paint dry.

4 To antique the
squares, paint over the
squares on one strip of
tape with black, including
the sides (see Photo B).
Moisten a paper towel in
water. Use the moist
paper towel to wipe off
most of the black paint
so the color shows
through. Antique one
strip of squares at a time.
Leave the black paint on

B

for a short time or it will
be hard to wipe off.

5 When the antiquing is
dry, apply a coat of gloss
varnish to all the squares.

6 Paint the front,
sides, and opening edges
of the papier-mâché
frame black.

7 Arrange the squares
first around the opening
of the frame and work
toward the outer edges.
When you are happy with
the arrangement, glue
the back of the squares
to the frame one at a
time. Let the glue dry.
Insert a photo of your
choice in the frame.

Household utensils make great stamping designs when you dip them into your favorite paint colors. No two shirts will ever be the same!

stamp-it fun shirt

YOU'LL NEED

Solid-color cotton shirt
Waxed paper; scissors
Fabric paints in your
   favorite colors
Paper plates
Plastic spoon
Kitchen utensils (we used
   two types of potato
   mashers, a cup, and a
   bottle sponge)
Printer paper

HERE'S HOW

1 Wash and dry your shirt before you stamp it. (DO NOT use any fabric softener or the paint may peel off.)

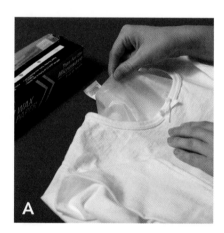

A

2 Cut pieces of waxed paper to fit inside the shirt body and sleeves. Slide the waxed paper pieces between the two layers of fabric as shown in Photo A, *below left,* to keep the fabric layers separated.

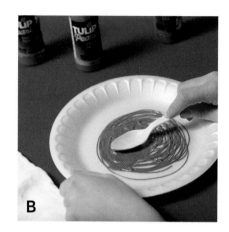

B

3 Squeeze one color of paint on each paper plate. Smooth out the paint using a plastic spoon as shown in Photo B. Dab a kitchen utensil in the paint. Before painting experiment on a piece of printer paper. Set the painted utensil on the paper and gently pull up. Try each utensil to decide which shapes are your favorites, then you're ready to start stamping your shirt.

GOOD IDEA
Use only metal or throwaway utensils because paint may ruin wood or plastic utensils.

C

4 Look at the shirt photograph, *opposite,* to make our pattern or make one of your own. If you wish, stamp one shape and one color on the body and sleeves of the shirt. Change utensils and paint colors and stamp more designs as shown in Photo C, sometimes slightly overlapping the designs.

5 Let the shirt lie flat while the paint dries. After the shirt is dry, remove the waxed paper.

friendship bracelets

Make a bracelet for yourself and one for a friend.
All you need is a zipper and your imagination!

YOU'LL NEED

6- or 7-inch zipper
Thick white crafts glue
Star jewels
Tube-style paint pens
Adhesive fasteners, such
as Velcro

HERE'S HOW

1 On the fabric part of the zipper, glue star jewels in a row or make a pattern. Let the glue dry.

2 Use paint pens to make fun designs on the zipper around the jewels. Or use the paint pens to write your friends' names.

GOOD IDEA
Sew beads or buttons on the zipper for decoration instead of gluing on jewels.

3 Wrap the zipper around your wrist to see where the zipper ends overlap. Cut the fastener pieces into small squares. Peel off the backing on the self-stick fastener and stick it to the ends of the zipper where they overlapped—two pieces on the right side and two pieces on the wrong side as shown in the photo, *above*.

GOOD IDEA
Instead of using adhesive fasteners to close your bracelet, sew on snaps.

65

Remind Dad how much he means to you with
this personalized baseball.

autographed
baseball

YOU'LL NEED

Baseball
Pencil
Paint markers in black
   and red
Candleholder
Colored wire or ribbon
Scissors

HERE'S HOW

1 Write a message on the baseball first with a pencil so you can erase any mistakes. Write over the pencil with paint markers. Let it dry. Draw hearts or other designs around the writing. Let it dry.

2 Place the baseball on a candleholder. Tie a colored wire or ribbon bow around the stem of the holder. Trim the ribbon or wire ends.

GOOD IDEA
Instead of candleholders, place the baseballs on curtain rings or mini cup trophies.

67

in-the-swim beach pail

This bright beach pail carries your gear to the shore, then holds found treasures to carry back home.

YOU'LL NEED

Pail
Acrylic paint; paintbrush
Pencil; tracing paper
Scissors; jumbo rickrack

HERE'S HOW

1 Paint the outside of the pail with a yellow stripe on the top and bottom and white in between. Let the paint dry.

2 Draw the patterns, *below*, onto tracing paper. Cut out. Trace around the shapes on the pail, looking at the photo, *opposite*, as a guide. For the zigzag, trace the edges of a piece of rickrack on the pencil. Paint in the details. Let the paint dry.

Trace the fish and bubble patterns to make your pail.

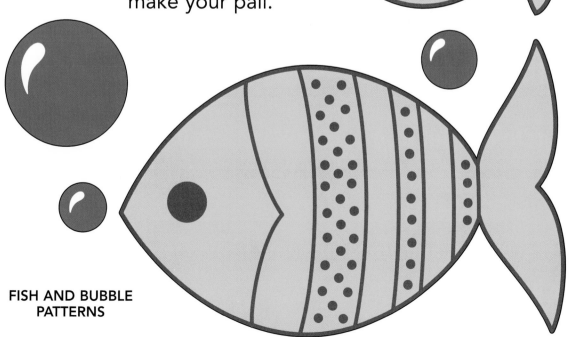

FISH AND BUBBLE PATTERNS

make some FUN

Snip it, fold it, cut it in two—paper is fun if you know what to do! Make a snowflake, a cricket, or a pinwheel to spin. Cut a garland or a box to put treasures in! Now get out some paper, scissors, and glue, for some fun paper crafts that are made by YOU!

with paper!

turtle racers

Be a good sport and have fun playing with tissue paper turtles.

YOU'LL NEED

**Sturdy dinner-size paper
plates; glue stick**

**3 sheets of colored
tissue paper**

**Crafting foam in any
color; scissors**

Sequins

Thick white crafts glue

Pencil

8-foot lengths of string

HERE'S HOW

1 Apply glue stick to the entire back of the paper plate. Place the lightest color of tissue paper on the glue and smooth out any air bubbles with your fingers.

2 Tear shapes out of contrasting colors of tissue paper. Apply glue stick over sections of the base color and lay the shapes on the glue.

3 Using the photo, *opposite*, as a guide, cut out four feet, a head, and a tail from crafting foam. Glue the ends of the foam pieces to the rim of the undecorated side of the plate. Let the glue dry.

4 Glue sequin eyes and nostrils to the head. With a pencil point, pierce a hole 2 inches below the plate rim in the center of the turtle's back.

5 Tie one string end around the bottom of a tree trunk or chair leg, 1 foot above the ground or floor. Thread the string through the hole in the turtle's back. Hold the end of the string in your hand and jiggle it up and down to get your turtle to walk on his feet all the way to the tree or chair. Play side by side with a friend to see whose turtle is faster.

paper plate pets

Let your imagination soar with crazy critters that can take any shape or form.

YOU'LL NEED

Paper plates
Marking pens
Tape
Construction paper
Scissors
Ruler
Thick white crafts glue
Large wiggle eyes or black and white paper, tin cans or plastic lids, and a pencil
Pom-poms

HERE'S HOW

1 For each puppet, color both sides of a paper plate with marking pens (or start with a colored plate). Fold the plate in half.

2 Tape the edges of a 4×1½-inch paper strip on top of the plate for your fingers and a 2×1½-inch strip on the bottom for your thumb.

3 Cut out paper feathers, teeth, a tongue, background for eyes, antennae, and any other features. Experiment with different shapes to make the creatures look scared, happy, or terrifying. Fold, bend, and curl the features as you like.

4 Arrange the paper features on the colored plate and glue them in place. Let the glue dry.

5 Glue on the wiggle eyes. If you don't have eyes large enough for this project, trace around cans or plastic lids and cut out eyes from white and black paper. Trace a large circle for the white eye and a smaller black circle for the pupil. Cut out the shapes. Glue the black circles to the bottom of the white circles or place the pupils in different places to make funny expressions.

6 Glue on pom-poms for the nostrils. Let the glue dry.

chirping cricket

Have a leapin' good time making these crickets chirp.

YOU'LL NEED

Cardboard tube; scissors
Green acrylic paint
Paintbrush
Tracing paper; pencil
Green crafting foam
Thick white crafts glue
Craft sticks or emery
  boards
Paper punch
Pipe cleaner
2 pom-poms
2 wiggly eyes

HERE'S HOW

1 To shape the tail, cut a diagonal wedge from one end of the tube. Cut a mouth shape on the bottom of the other end of the tube. Paint the tube green and let it dry.

Trace these patterns to make your cricket pal!

2 Trace the patterns onto tracing paper. Trace around the leg pattern two times and the arm pattern once on foam. Glue the arms under the cricket behind the mouth. Glue the legs to each side of the tube. Glue an emery board or craft stick to the cricket's legs.

3 Punch two holes on top of the tube for antennae. Fold the pipe cleaner in half and thread the ends through the holes. Glue the pom-poms to the tube rim. Glue wiggle eyes on the pom-poms. To make the cricket chirp, rub a craft stick across the textured surface on the legs.

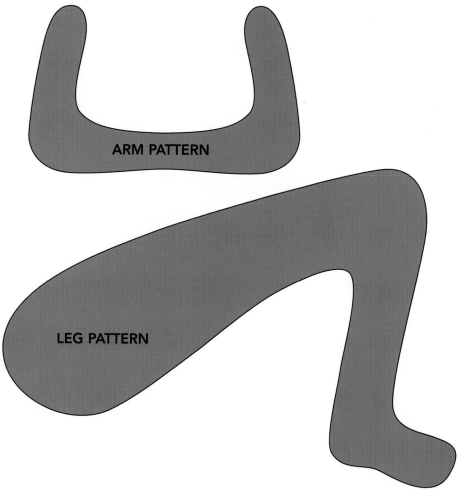

ARM PATTERN

LEG PATTERN

Sparkly

Snowflakes

Create your own glittering white snowflakes any time of the year! These three-dimensional sparkly paper snowflakes are like the icy cold kind—no two will ever be the same. Turn the page to learn how to make them.

sparkly snowflakes

YOU'LL NEED

Lightweight printer
   paper
Scissors; ruler; pencil
Lightweight string
Glue stick; white glitter

HERE'S HOW

1 Fold the sheet of paper in half, with the long edges together.

2 Unfold the paper and cut along the fold line.

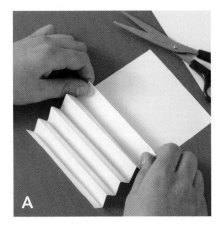

3 Start at the short end and fold the paper like a fan every ¾ inch as shown in Photo A, *above*.

GOOD IDEA
Display snowflakes by tucking in a wreath, scattering on a table, or hanging on a tree.

4 Trace a pattern, *opposite*, on one end of the paper or draw your own snowflake design.

5 Cut out the center notch as shown on the

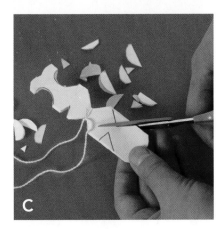

patterns and in Photo B. Tie a piece of string around the notch.

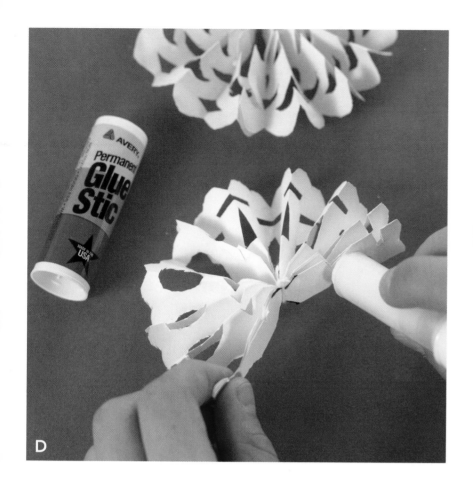

Trace these cool snowflake patterns!

6 Cut out the black sections of the snowflake as shown on the pattern and in Photo C.

7 Glue the paper ends together as shown in Photo D. Trim the string ends or use the string to hang the snowflake.

8 Glue glitter to the snowflake edges or on the front of the snowflake.

Remember to fold along the dotted lines!

pinwheel pizzazz

Now you can make your own special pinwheel–in the colors you choose– and play for hours outside in the wind. Try to make one–it's a breeze!

HERE'S HOW

1 With a pencil and ruler, mark an 8-inch square on the back side of the wrapping paper. Cut out the square.

2 Draw lines from corner to corner on the back of the paper as shown in Photo A, *opposite.*

3 Place the penny in the center of the "X" on the back of the wrapping paper and draw around it.

YOU'LL NEED

Piece of wrapping paper
Pencil; ruler; scissors
A penny
12-inch piece of
  ¼-inch-square
  balsa wood
Marking pens
Curling ribbons to match
  wrapping paper
Straight pin with large
  plastic head
Large pony bead
Eraser from end of pencil

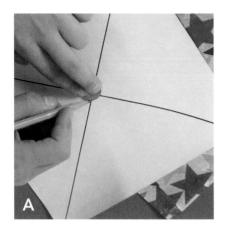

A

4 Fold all four corners to the center and crease the folds (see Photo B).

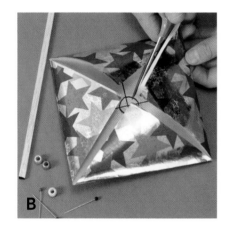

B

5 Use scissors to cut between the folded triangles as shown in Photo B. Be careful to cut up to, but NOT THROUGH the center circle. (You'll have four cuts when finished.)

6 Decorate the wood piece for the handle however you wish using marking pens as shown in Photo C, *above right*.

C

7 Cut eight pieces of curling ribbon, each about 8 inches long. Ask a grown-up to use scissors to curl the ends.

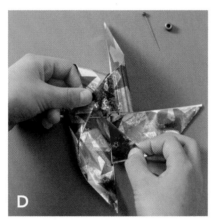

D

8 Bend (DO NOT FOLD) every other point to the center of the square as shown in Photo D.

9 One at a time, push the pin through the center of the curling ribbons, then through all four points of the pinwheel. Push the pin through the center of the square.

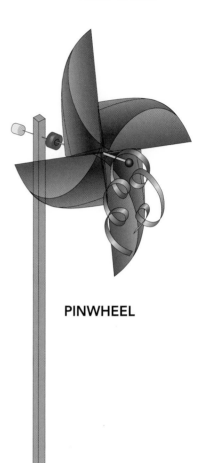

Put your pinwheel together like this!

PINWHEEL

10 Place a pony bead on the pin behind the pinwheel. Next push the pin through one end of the wood handle, about ½ inch from the end. Carefully push the eraser onto the end of the pin.

11 If you like, decorate the pinwheel blades with stickers and more ribbon.

treasure boxes

Hide secret treasures inside these special paper boxes you can make yourself. Try all kinds of papers and see the boxes take shape.

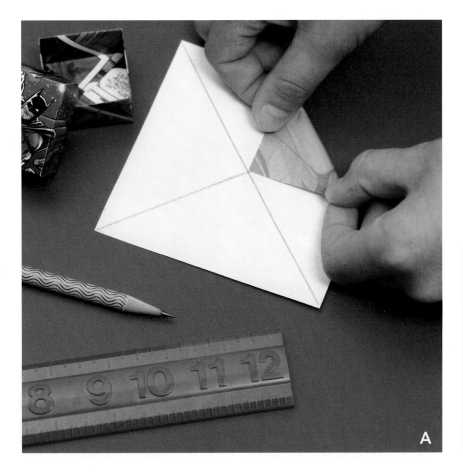

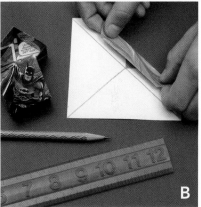

YOU'LL NEED

Medium-weight craft
   paper, comic books,
   or magazines
Ruler
Pencil
Scissors
Thick white crafts glue
Decorations for box
   top such as jewels
   and stickers

HERE'S HOW

1 Measure and cut out
one 4½-inch square for
the box top and one
4¼-inch square for the
box bottom.

2 Draw an X across the
back of both squares,
corner to corner.

3 On one paper square,
fold a corner to the center
of the X as shown in
Photo A, *above*.

4 Fold the same section
again (see Photo B) to the
center line. Unfold the
paper and repeat with each
of the other three corners.

continued on page 86

GOOD IDEA
Be sure to crease
the folds with your
fingernail so
they are easy
to see.

treasure boxes

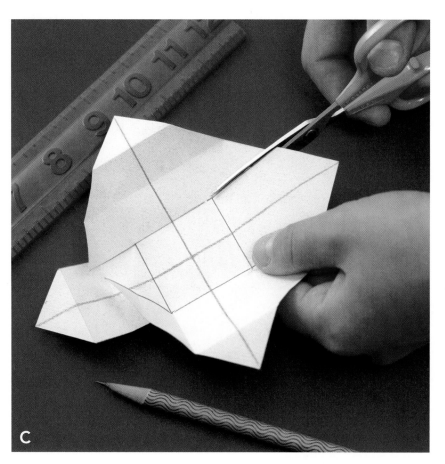

C

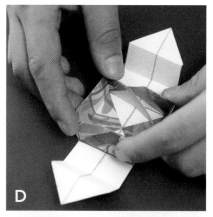

D

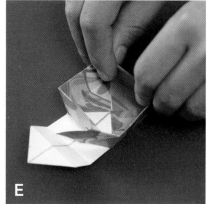

E

5 Repeat Step 3 and Step 4 to make the second paper square.

6 For both paper squares, refer to the diagrams *opposite* and Photo C. Make four cuts into the square along the fold lines (they are drawn in so you can see them better). Be sure not to cut into the blue center square that is shown on the diagram!

7 Fold in the side triangles and bend the corners to form the sides of the box (see Photo D).

GOOD IDEA
Do not cut into the center square because it will become the top or bottom of the box.

8 Fold the other two sections over the sides and tuck them in on the inside of the box as shown in Photo E. Use a dab of glue to hold it.

9 Decorate the top of the box if you like, using glue to attach any jewels. Put the lid on the bottom of the box.

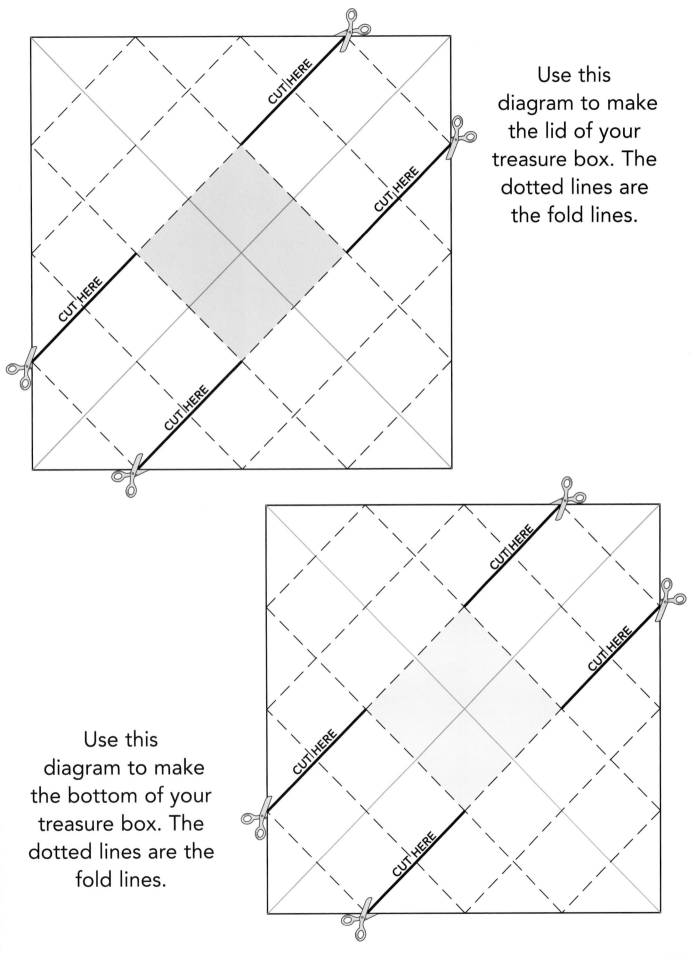

Use this diagram to make the lid of your treasure box. The dotted lines are the fold lines.

Use this diagram to make the bottom of your treasure box. The dotted lines are the fold lines.

CUT HERE

CUT HERE

CUT HERE

CUT HERE

CUT HERE

CUT HERE

CUT HERE

CUT HERE

magic garlands

With long, narrow paper and just a snip of your scissors, you can create magic garlands to trim plain stationery or to use for decorating!

YOU'LL NEED

Pencil

White printer paper

Paper to make the
garlands: streamer,
adding machine, or
printer paper

Scissors

Pinking shears or
scallop-edge scissors,
if you wish

Round paper punches

HERE'S HOW

1 Trace a pattern from
pages 90–91 on
printer paper. Color in the
black areas with pencil.
Cut out the traced pattern
around the four edges.

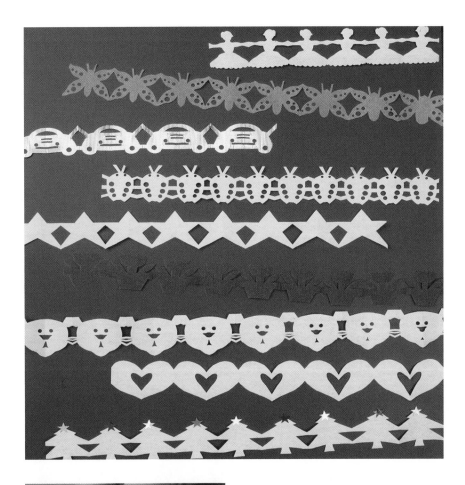

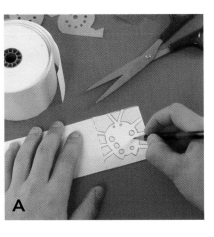

A

2 Lay the pattern under
the garland paper and
match the edge to the
end of the strip. Trace the

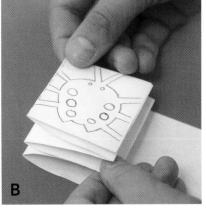

B

pattern on the end of the
strip as shown in Photo A.

3 Where the design ends,
fold the paper like a fan,
keeping the edges even as
you fold (see Photo B).
Fold as many times as you
wish (not too many though,
or it is hard to cut).

4 Trim the top (unfolded
edge) of the paper with
pinking shears if making
the flower. Trim the bottom
with scallop-edge scissors
if making the dancer.

continued on page 90

GOOD IDEA
If you use plain
paper, cut it into
strips about
2¼×11 inches.

magic garlands

C

Have fun tracing these patterns to make paper garlands!

FOLD

FOLD

FOLD

TREE

5 Use the pencil lines as a guide. Cut away the areas between the lines shown as the dark areas on the pattern and in Photo C.

6 If the pattern has small round dots in the design, punch these out last using paper punches.

GOOD IDEA
The trick to making garlands is to be sure both sides have some uncut folds.

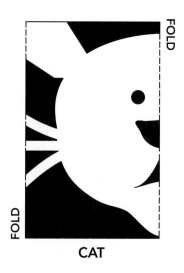

FOLD

FOLD

CAT

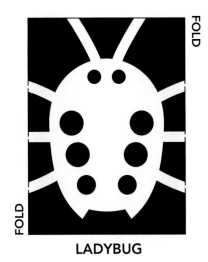

LADYBUG

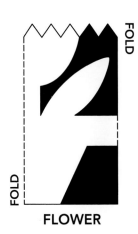

FLOWER

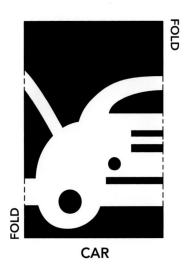

CAR

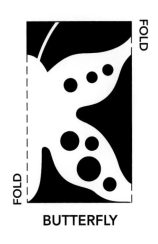

BUTTERFLY

Remember,
the dotted lines
are the fold lines—
don't cut them!

HEART

DANCER

SNOWMAN

STAR

91

Bart-the-bird piñata

It's always such fun to have a party
with a new friend, and Bart-the-bird
piñata will be happy to bring lots
of candy for you and
all your friends!

YOU'LL NEED

About 1 cup of water
About 1 cup of flour
Container to hold the
    water and flour mixture
Newspapers
Large oval-shape balloon
Black marker
Wide masking tape
Wrapped candy
Acrylic or tempera paint
    in white and black
Paintbrush
3 packages of yellow
    tissue paper (in all one
    color or multicolored
    yellows); scissors
Pencil with new eraser
Thick white crafts glue
Disposable plate
Printer paper
Three 8½×11-inch pieces
    of orange construction
    paper; yellow feathers

HERE'S HOW

1 Measure about 1 cup of water and pour it into the container. Measure and add about 1 cup of flour to the water. Mix the water and flour.

2 Tear or cut the newspaper into strips that are about 1½ inches wide.

3 Blow up the balloon and tie it. With a black marker, draw a circle on the bottom about 3 inches in diameter to help you remember to leave this hole uncovered.

continued on page 94

93

Bart-the-bird piñata

A

B

6 If you want your piñata to be extra-strong, apply a third coat. Always be sure to leave the hole uncovered. The balloon may begin to shrink a little, but that's all right.

4 Dip each newspaper strip into the flour mixture and put it on the balloon as shown in Photo A, *above*. Cover the entire balloon with strips of paper going in all directions, except leave the hole you marked uncovered. Let this layer dry.

5 After the first layer is dry, make the eyes by wadding up two little pieces of newspaper about the size of a golf ball. Tape these to the dry papier-mâché with masking tape where you want the eyes to be (see Photo B). Now start the second layer of papier-mâché by dipping the newspaper into the flour mixture and placing it over the eyes and all over the balloon again, remembering not to cover the hole at the bottom. Allow this layer to dry.

C

7 After the last layer is dry, pop the balloon. Reach in the hole and pull out the balloon. Fill the papier-mâché sphere with wrapped candies and tape over the hole securely with masking tape as shown in Photo C.

D

8 Paint the eyes white. Paint a large black circle in the center of the piñata as shown in Photo D. This is where the beak will go after the tissue paper is on the piñata. Put a black dot in the middle of the eye and a white dot highlight.

9 Cut the tissue paper into 2 inch squares. It does not matter if these are not cut perfectly. The size can vary a little. You will need at least 100 squares, so cut several of them at once. With good scissors, you can layer about five or six pieces of tissue paper at a time and cut through all of the layers.

10 Mark a 3-inch circle on the black painted space. You will not cover this part because the beak will go here when you are done. Also leave an area without tissue paper at the bottom of the bird where the tape is (about a 3-inch circle) so you can glue the feet to the bottom of the bird.

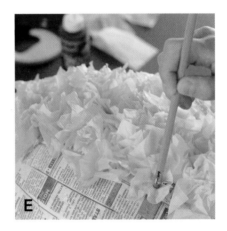

E

11 You are now ready to cover your piñata with tissue squares. To make fluffy tissue feathers, put some glue on a disposable plate. Use the eraser end of the pencil to wrap a tissue square around the pencil and dip it into the glue. Put the pencil with the tissue and glue onto the piñata as shown in Photo E. Repeat this step, placing the little pieces close together.

It will take a lot of time to cover the whole balloon. Remember to leave the spots for the beak and feet.

F

12 Trace the beak and feet patterns on *pages 96–97* onto printer paper and cut them out. Lay these patterns on the orange paper and cut out two feet and two beak pieces.

13 Fold the beak pieces as marked on the pattern. Glue the beak pieces on the piñata on the black paint without tissue paper (see Photo F). Glue the feet to the bottom of the bird where you left a spot. Glue some feathers on his head in between some of the tissue.

continued on page 96

95

Bart-the-bird piñata

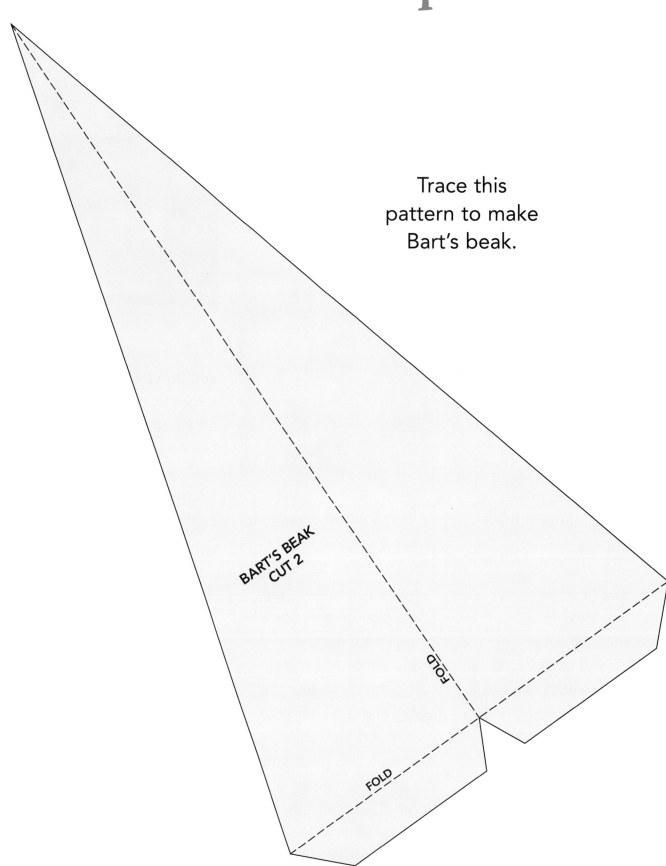

Trace this
pattern to make
Bart's beak.

BART'S BEAK
CUT 2

FOLD

FOLD

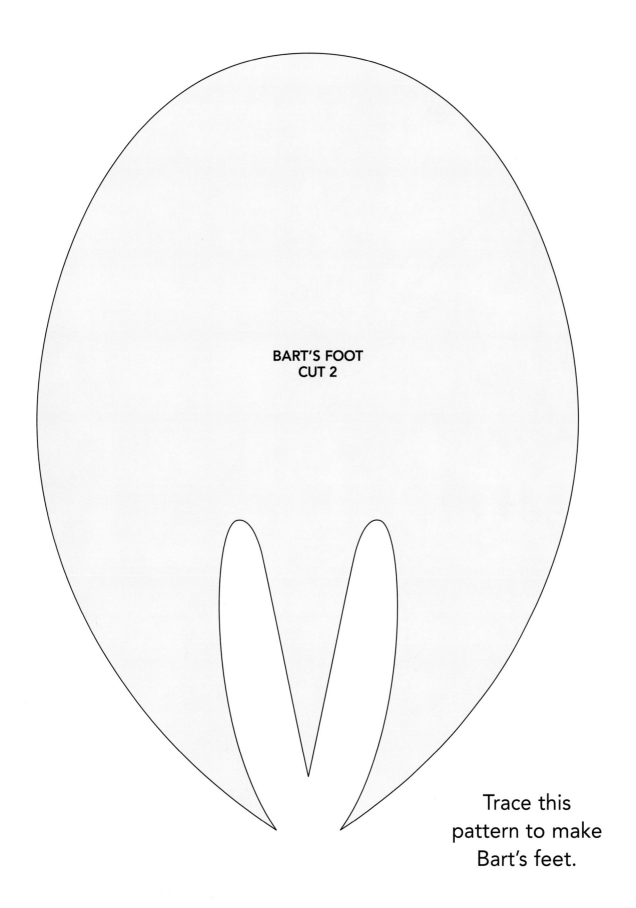

BART'S FOOT
CUT 2

Trace this
pattern to make
Bart's feet.

Want to see more of your friends? Now you can see them every day as they smile at you on frames, lampshades, and note cards.

Picture Pals

How to get copies of your photos and make a collage:

HERE'S HOW

1 Cut out pictures of your friends from school pictures or snapshots. (If you don't want to cut up your photos, copy the entire snapshot and trim the copy. For multiple projects copy the trimmed copy.)

2 Arrange and overlap pictures, turning some upside down and sideways, on a piece of printer paper. (It's OK if some of the paper shows through.)

3 Use a glue stick to hold the pictures in place.

4 Ask a grown-up to take you to a photocopy store and make several black-and-white copies of your photo collage. (You may have to lighten the contrast of the machine. It's easy to do—just ask for help.)

continued on page 100

99

picture pal projects

Picture Frame

YOU'LL NEED

Thick white crafts glue
8×10-inch oval photo mat
  with cardboard backing
Copied black and white
  photo collage; scissors
Decoupage medium,
  such as Mod Podge
Paintbrush
Tape
Colorful rubber bands
Printer paper
Pencil
9×4-inch piece of
  medium-weight
  cardboard for stand

HERE'S HOW

1 Apply the glue evenly to the front of the photo mat. Lay the photo collage, right side up, over the mat and smooth it in place with your fingers.

A

2 Trim away any excess paper from around the outside edge and inside the oval opening as shown in Photo A, *above*. Let dry.

3 Paint on several coats of decoupage medium over the collage (see Photo B). Let it dry between coats.

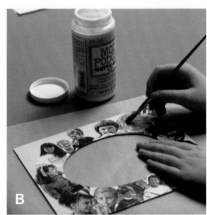

B

C

4 Place the oval mat over the picture to be framed. Tape the picture in place at the top edge on the back.

5 Place the backing cardboard behind the picture. Use rubber bands to hold the layers in place.

6 Trace the photo stand pattern on *page 103* onto printer paper; cut it out. Draw around the pattern on the medium-weight piece of cardboard and cut it out.

7 Fold the stand as shown on the pattern.

8 Center the stand on the back of the frame. Matching the stand bottom to the bottom edge of the frame, glue down the tabs as shown in Photo C.

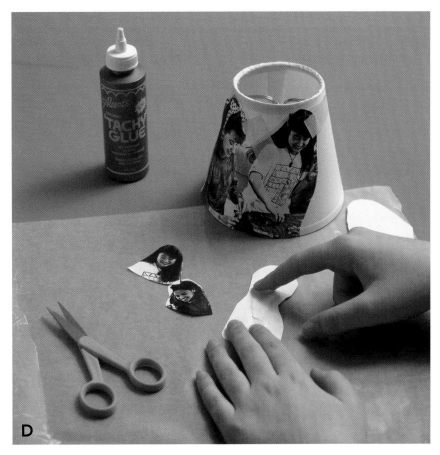

D

Lampshade

YOU'LL NEED

Copied black and white photo collage; scissors
Small lampshade with smooth surface
Magic tape, such as Scotch or 3M
Printer paper
Thick white crafts glue
Decoupage medium, such as Mod Podge
Paintbrush
Black single-edge bias tape

HERE'S HOW

1 Cut apart the photo collage. Arrange the pieces on the lampshade. Tape them in place.

2 When the shade is covered, remove one piece at a time. Place each piece face down on a piece of clean printer paper and apply glue evenly over the back of each piece (see Photo D).

continued on page 102

picture pal projects

3 Press each glued piece onto the shade and smooth it with your fingers to be sure that all edges are glued down. Use a clean piece of paper for each gluing.

4 Allow the shade to dry completely. Use a paintbrush to cover it with several coats of decoupage medium, letting it dry between coats.

5 Glue a strip of black bias tape around the top edge of the lampshade, overlapping the ends of the tape at the back of the shade.

Note Card

YOU'LL NEED

Copied black and white
  photo collage
Glue stick
Scissors
9×6-inch piece of
  paper folded to a
  4½×6-inch card
Colored pencils

HERE'S HOW

1 Cut a shape from the photo collage that is at least ½ inch smaller than the size of the card front. Use a glue stick to glue the collage to the note card.

2 Use colored pencils to color in whatever areas you would like on your photo collage as shown *above*. Use unusual colors—like blue or green for hair!

To make your
photo stand, trace
this pattern onto
printer paper and
cut it out.

Draw around the
pattern on the
medium-weight
piece of cardboard
and cut out.

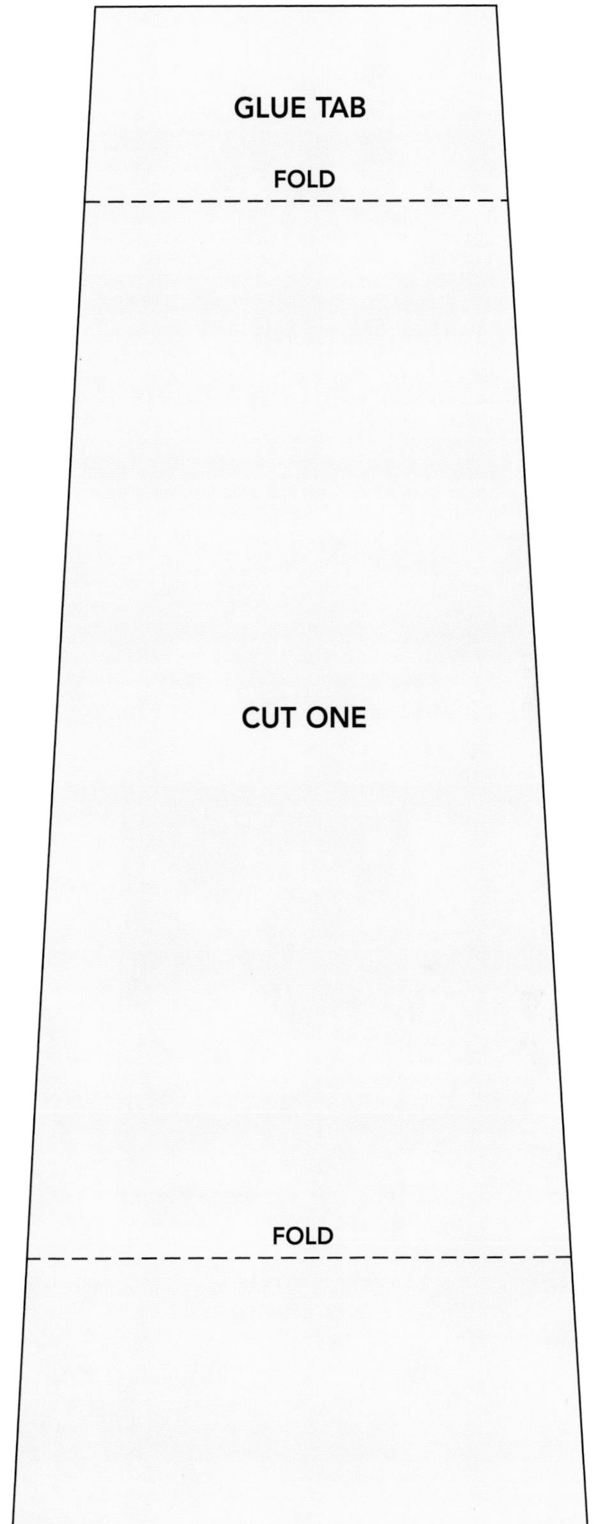

GLUE TAB

FOLD

CUT ONE

FOLD

GLUE TAB

pet frame

Show off photos of your finicky feline or playful pooch in a frame that is created just for your pet.

YOU'LL NEED

Computer and printer
Scissors
Magazines
Newspapers
Glue stick
Printer paper
Decoupage medium,
  such as Mod Podge
Paintbrush
Frame
Picture mat, if you want

HERE'S HOW

1 Use your computer to print out words, such as cat, dog, or friends, in different fonts, sizes, and colors. If you don't have a computer, clip out words from magazines and newspapers. If you want more than one copy, glue the word(s) on a piece of paper and have copies made at a copy center.

2 To include photos or pictures, clip them out of magazines or have color copies made of your own photos.

3 Cover your work surface with newspapers. To decoupage the words or pictures on a frame, trim the pieces as you like and decide where you want to put them. Brush decoupage medium over the frame. To add cutouts, brush the back side with decoupage medium and smooth onto the frame or mat. Wrap the cutouts around the center opening and edges. Overlap pieces as you wish. Continue adding cutouts until the entire frame or mat is covered. Let the decoupage medium dry.

4 Before applying decoupage medium over the cutouts, test it on an extra cutout to be sure it doesn't make the colors run together. If it doesn't, paint decoupage medium over all of the cutouts. Let it dry.

cool paper book covers

batiked
paper

For a great after-school project, decorate paper with different techniques, then cover your notebooks and textbooks with your creations.

YOU'LL NEED

Paper grocery bag
Scissors
Thick crayons
Bucket of water
Watercolor paints
Paper towels
Finger paint
Construction paper
Sponge
Comb
Paintbrush
Corrugated cardboard
Cutout shapes
Book
Ruler
Tape

HERE'S HOW

1 To make batiked paper, cut a brown paper grocery bag along one fold. Cut off the bottom and flatten the bag. With thick crayons, color geometric designs all over the bag (light, bright colors work the best). Crumple the bag and place it in a bucket of water to create crackle lines. Gently squeeze the bag, lay it flat, and let it dry. Brush dark watercolor paints over the crayon. Blot with paper towels if needed. Let the paint dry.

GOOD IDEA
Use these pretty handmade papers as giftwrap for extra-special presents!

continued on page 108

107

These photos help show how to make the swirly paper.

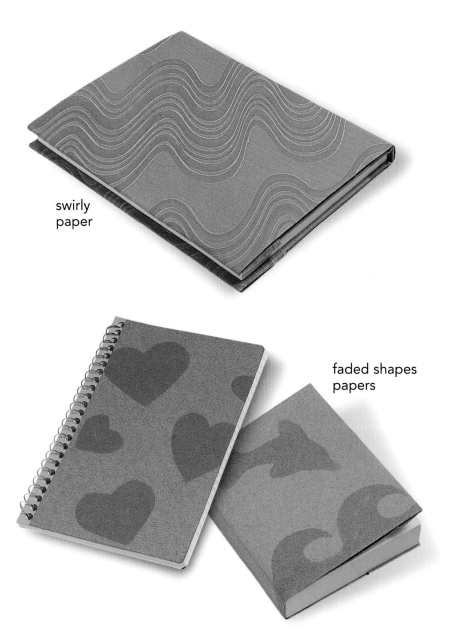

swirly
paper

faded shapes
papers

2 **To make swirly paper,** glob finger paint onto a sheet of construction paper as shown in Photo A, *above*. Spread out paint using a sponge (see Photo B). Use a comb (see Photo C), a paintbrush, a piece of cardboard with notches cut into it, or another tool to create patterns on the paper. Let the paint dry.

3 **To make faded-shapes paper,** lay construction paper on a patio or porch on a sunny day. Place a variety of objects or cutouts on the paper. Return in a few hours to see how the paper has faded.

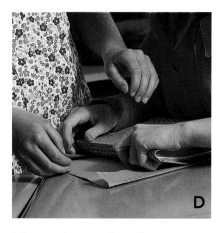  

These photos show how to wrap your book.

4 **To wrap your book,** lay the paper, plain side up, on a flat surface. Open the book and put it with its spine in the middle of the paper. The paper should be at least 2 inches bigger than the book all the way around.

5 Make a crease along the top of the book the length of the paper. Make another crease along the bottom of the book. Fold the paper in along both creases as shown in Photos D and E.

6 Keep the book closed and crease the paper again along the edges of the book front and back covers. Fold in the paper along these creases too. Slip the front cover into the end pocket formed by folding the paper. Do the same with the back cover as shown in Photo F. If needed, readjust the creases to get a better fit. Tape the end flaps to the outside paper if you want.

GOOD IDEA
Use alphabet stickers to add your name or other words to a book cover.

GOOD IDEA
Buy a plain journal or diary and wrap it with your personalized paper.

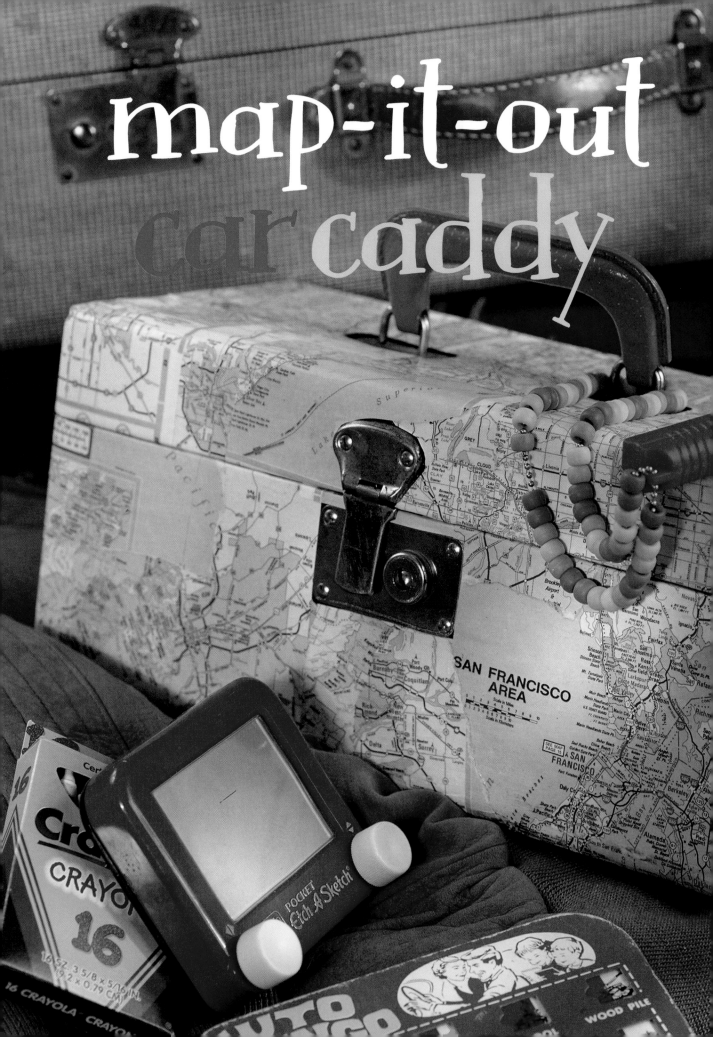

map-it-out
car caddy

Just the right size for your travel games, maps, and car snacks, these take-along totes are a world of fun to make.

YOU'LL NEED

Maps or old atlas
Scissors
Glossy decoupage
   medium, such as
   Mod Podge
Paintbrush
Carrying case, small
   toolbox, or other
   small case
Neck chain
Pony beads in colors
   you like
Small flashlight

HERE'S HOW

1 Use scissors to cut sections from maps or pages from an atlas. To apply each piece to the case, coat the back side with decoupage medium. Place the pieces on the case, trimming as necessary to fit around the hardware. Line up the straight edges with the edges of the case that meet. Cover the entire case with map sections. Let the decoupage medium dry.

2 Brush a top coat of decoupage medium over all mapped areas. Let it dry. Apply another coat if you want and let dry.

3 String pony beads on the neck chain. Thread the chain through a hole in the flashlight handle and attach it to the case handle.

let's have some

They're jolly, spooky, and really neat. These holiday projects don't miss a beat! From trick-or-treating to holiday greetings, will-you-be-mine to Easter egg time, you'll have lots to make, don't you fear, no matter what the time of year!

holiday FUN!

dressed-up pumpKins

Create one-of-a-kind no-carve pumpkin people with a variety of items from around the house.

For the glamour girl

Pumpkin
Artificial eyelashes
Acrylic paint in red and
    pink; paintbrush
Thick white crafts glue
Red raffia
Straw hat; ribbon
Silk flowers

For the cowboy

Pumpkin
Orange foam ball
Scissors
Thick white crafts glue
Acrylic paint in black,
    white, and yellow
Paintbrush
Cowboy hat
2 bandannas
Toy sheriff's badge

For the veggie lady

Pumpkin
Quilting pins
Lettuce
Black olives
Yellow peppers
Sweet red peppers
Hot-glue gun and
    hot-glue sticks
Thread; needle

HERE'S HOW

1 Wash the pumpkin. Let it dry. Trim the stem short if it is too long.

2 **For the glamour girl,** remove backing from artificial eyelashes and press the eyelashes on the pumpkin. Use acrylic paint to add a nose, cheeks, and a mouth. Let the paint dry. Glue raffia to the inside of the hat to look like hair. Glue a ribbon around the hat. Add silk flowers. Set the hat on the pumpkin.

3 **For the cowboy,** cut a foam ball in half. Glue the flat side of one half to the center of the pumpkin. Use acrylic paint to add eyes and a mouth. Let the paint dry. Add a white highlight to the nose and eyes. Tie a bandanna around the cowboy hat and put the hat on the pumpkin. Tie the other bandanna around the bottom of the pumpkin and hold it in place with the sheriff's badge.

4 **For the veggie lady,** pin lettuce on top of the pumpkin for hair. Stick on olive eyes, a yellow pepper nose, and sweet red pepper ears and mouth. Stick on yellow pepper earrings. Glue the veggies in place with hot glue. For a necklace, string olives on thread and put it around the bottom of the pumpkin.

Spellbound pumpkin

Decorate a "spooktacular" pumpkin with words made from alphabet macaroni.

YOU'LL NEED

Pumpkin
Alphabet macaroni
Paintbrush
Glossy decoupage
  medium, such as
  Mod Podge
Acrylic metallic paint
  in copper, green,
  purple, gold, or
  other colors
Pencil with round-tip
  eraser

HERE'S HOW

1 Decide what words or phrases to put on the pumpkin. Find the macaroni letters. On the pumpkin, paint a line of decoupage medium where you want the words. Place the letters on the decoupage medium. Let the words stick to the pumpkin.

2 Paint the dried letters lightly with metallic paint. Use only one color on the entire word or phrase so it stands out. Let the paint dry.

3 To make dots, dip the eraser end of the pencil in copper paint. Carefully dot the paint on the pumpkin where you want. Let the paint dry.

GOOD IDEA

For greeting cards glue alphabet macaroni on folded colored paper to spell messages.

carnival
pumpkin

*You'll have to get your fingers wet to leave
your mark on this colorful pumpkin!*

YOU'LL NEED

Pumpkin
Newspapers
**Acrylic enamel paint
in bright colors**
Flat paintbrush

HERE'S HOW

1 Wash and dry the
pumpkin. Cover the work
surface with newspapers.

2 Paint a wide zigzag
stripe around the middle
of the pumpkin. Paint
wide stripes from the
bottom of the zigzag to
the bottom of the
pumpkin. Use a flat
paintbrush to paint
small squares on the top
of the pumpkin. Let the
paint dry.

3 Use your finger to
make dots on the zigzag
stripe. Let the paint dry.

119

Surprise family and friends with these clever pouches that are made from foam and held together with tiny round eyelets.

PUMPKIN
POUCH
PATTERN

treat-filled
pouches

YOU'LL NEED

Tracing paper; pencil
Scissors and pinking
   shears, if desired
Crafting foam in yellow,
   orange, white, and
   purple
Awl; eyelets and an
   eyelet tool
Black permanent
   marking pen

HERE'S HOW

1 Trace one of the patterns, *opposite* or *right*, onto tracing paper. Cut out the pattern. Trace around the pattern pieces on the matching colors of foam. Cut out the shapes with scissors or pinking shears.

2 Layer the shapes as shown. Ask a grown-up to use an awl to make impressions through all the foam layers where grommets are to be. Take the piece apart and punch holes where the awl made a dent.

3 Layer the foam pieces and put an eyelet through each set of holes. Use the eyelet tool to make sure they are in place.

4 Draw in the ghost's face and write a name on the pocket with a black permanent marking pen.

GHOST POUCH PATTERN

121

family
disguises

You'll have everyone guessing who you are this Halloween with these fun disguises that are a breeze to make.

Goldie Locks

YOU'LL NEED

Scissors; yellow yarn
Yardstick
Plastic headband
Thick white crafts glue
2 yards of 1-inch-wide
   plaid ribbon

HERE'S HOW

1 Cut about 48 nine-inch
lengths of yarn for bangs.
Fold two strands at a time
in half. Place the loop
under the center of the
headband. Thread the
yarn ends through the
loop and pull tight.
Continue working on
both sides of the first yarn
until bang area is done.
Dab glue under the yarn
at both ends to hold it
in place.

2 For pigtails, cut
about 100 three-foot
lengths of yarn. With the
ends even, tie a piece of
yarn tightly in the center,
then tie it around center
of the headband.

3 Cut the ribbon into
four equal lengths. Tie a
pair of ribbons around
long lengths of yarn,
about 10 inches from the
ends. Do the same to
make the other side.

Silly Clown

YOU'LL NEED

Red plastic funnel about
   8 inches in diameter
Round white stickers
6 green pipe cleaners in
   varying widths
Hot-glue gun and
   hot-glue sticks
Tracing paper
Pencil
Scissors
Bright color felt scraps
Bright color pom-poms
20-inch length of
   1-inch-wide
   polka-dot ribbon
20 white paper
   coffee filters
Wide red marker
Paper punch
Cord

HERE'S HOW

1 If you can't find a red
funnel, ask a grown-up to
use red spray paint to
cover the outside surface.
Let the paint dry. Stick on
round white stickers
however you wish.

2 Cut the pipe cleaners
into lengths between
6 and 12 inches long.
Group the pipe cleaners
together and wind them
at the base. Hot-glue the
group of pipe cleaners to
the inside of the narrow
end of the funnel.

3 Trace the flower and
leaf patterns, *page 127*,
onto a piece of tracing

continued on page 124

123

family disguises

paper. Cut them out and trace onto felt. Cut small flowers from felt. Snip a tiny hole in the center, insert a pipe cleaner stem, and attach the flower on a pipe cleaner stem with hot glue. Glue it on the center pom-pom. Tie a leaf around the stem.

4 Glue a ribbon inside each side of the funnel for ties.

5 To make a collar, stack 18 to 20 coffee filters. Color around the edge of stacked filters with a wide red marker.

6 Separate the filters. Fold each filter in half. Punch a hole in the center about ½ inch from the fold.

7 Keep the filters folded and string all onto a cord. Ask a grown-up to help you put on the collar.

Grandpa Gus

YOU'LL NEED

Tracing paper
Pencil
Scissors
Long gray fake fur
Extra strong hair gel
Comb
Fine thread
Double-sided tape

GOOD IDEA
Remove the lenses from sunglasses to use when dressing up for Halloween or make believe!

HERE'S HOW

1 Ask a grown-up to help you enlarge and trace the patterns, *page 126*. Cut them out and trace them onto the back side of fake fur. Cut out the pieces.

2 Work enough hair gel into each piece to soak it. Shape each piece with your fingers. Twist the ends of the eyebrows and mustache into narrow points. Comb the hair in whatever shape you want.

3 Tie a piece of thread tightly in the center of the mustache. Cut off extra thread. On the gray hair, turn in the edges and hot-glue them to the back.

4 Use double-sided tape to stick the hair pieces to your head.

Miss America

YOU'LL NEED

Tracing paper
Pencil
Scissors
Crafting foam
White headband
Hot-glue gun and
   hot-glue sticks
Newspapers
White glue
Silver glitter; gems
Beads or sequins on
   a string
2½-inch-wide
   gold ribbon
White paper
Spray adhesive

HERE'S HOW

1 For a crown, trace the pattern, *page 127*, onto tracing paper. Cut out the pattern. Trace around the pattern onto foam and cut it out.

2 Center the foam piece on the headband and glue it in place with hot glue. Let the glue set.

3 Cover the work surface with newspapers. Coat the entire front of the foam piece with lots of white glue. While it is wet, sprinkle glitter on the glue. Shake off the extra and let the glue dry. Add gems and trim with hot glue.

4 For a banner, ask a grown-up to help you cut a piece of ribbon to fit around your shoulder and down to the opposite hip. Print "Miss America" on white paper. Keep the words together and cut out the strip. Cut more strips of plain white paper to fit along the whole ribbon.

5 Ask a grown-up to spray adhesive on the back side of the trimmed white paper strips. Let the spray dry until it is tacky. Stick the paper on the ribbon. Glue the ribbon ends together with hot glue to make a loop.

family disguises

Grandma Gracie

YOU'LL NEED

Gray yarn
Scissors
Plastic headband
Thick white crafts glue
Curlers
Bandanna or scarf
Tracing paper
Pencil
Purple crafting foam
Gems; ruler
Cold cream, if you want

HERE'S HOW

1 For the hair, cut groups of yarn from 10 to 36 inches long. Keep same lengths together and work with four strands at a time.

Fold the group of strands in half. Place the loop under the headband. Thread the yarn ends through the loop and pull tight. Continue adding yarn to the headband until it is completely covered. Dab glue under the yarn at both ends to hold it in place.

2 Cut three 12-inch lengths of yarn. Attach to the center of headband like you did the hair, except have tails end on the other side of the headband for bangs.

3 Wrap all the equal lengths of yarn in curlers.

4 To wear the hair, place the headband on and adjust the curlers to cover your head. Fold a bandanna in half with points together. Fold the point toward the center. Tie the bandanna around your neck.

5 For the glasses, trace the pattern, *opposite*. Cut it out from purple crafting foam. Cut two ¼-inch slits in the glasses front as shown on the pattern. Glue gems across the top of the frame. Let the glue dry. Push the ends of the glasses bows through slits in the frame front.

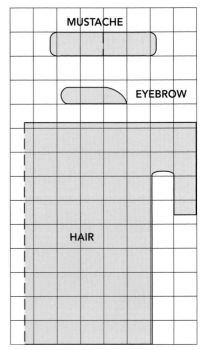

MUSTACHE

EYEBROW

HAIR

GRANDPA GUS PATTERNS   1 SQUARE = 1 INCH

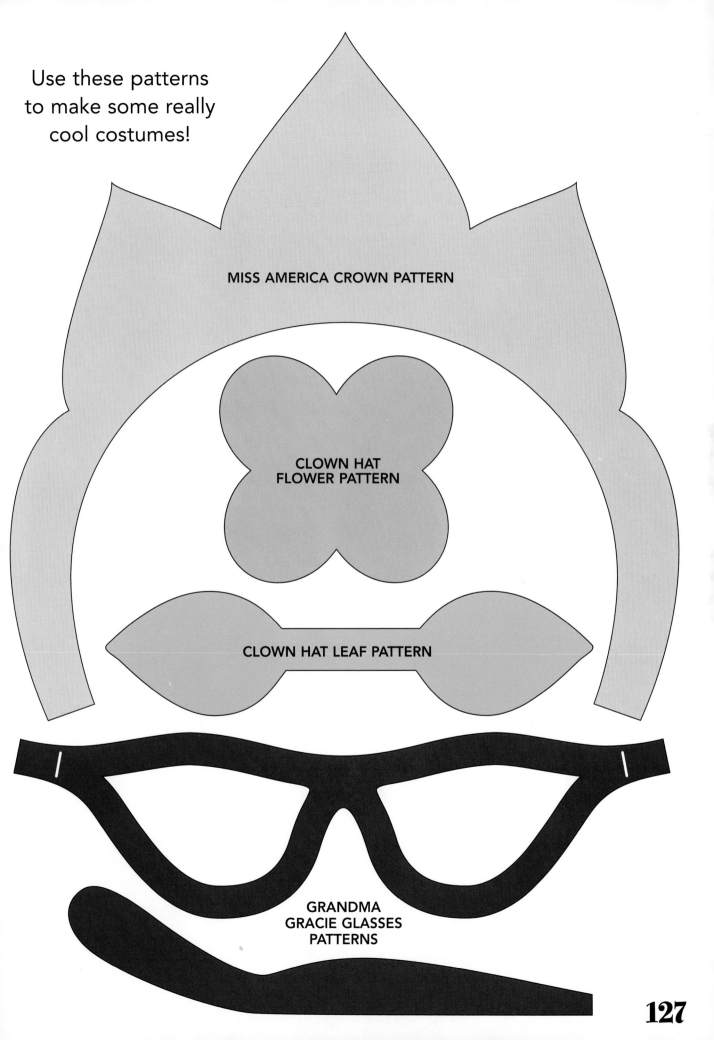

Use these patterns to make some really cool costumes!

MISS AMERICA CROWN PATTERN

CLOWN HAT
FLOWER PATTERN

CLOWN HAT LEAF PATTERN

GRANDMA
GRACIE GLASSES
PATTERNS

127

good manners napkins

Place a pretty napkin on your lap to remind you to use good manners.

YOU'LL NEED

Purchased cloth napkins
Large pieces of paper
Scissors
Pencil
Fabric markers

HERE'S HOW

1 Choose a phrase to write (such as "chew with your mouth closed," "use your napkin," or "use your manners") on the napkin. Cut a strip of paper the length of the napkin. Use a pencil to write the phrase on the paper.

2 Use the paper strip as a guide to write the phrase on each edge of the napkin with a fabric marker. Print with neat printing. At the end of each line in a letter, make a contrasting color dot.

GOOD IDEA

Use this idea to write polite reminders on cloth place mats and tablecloths.

129

pilgrim cap place cards

Welcome Thanksgiving guests with these delightful pilgrim cap place cards.

YOU'LL NEED

3-inch terra-cotta
    flowerpot
Acrylic paint in black,
    white, red, green,
    and blue; paintbrush
Crafting foam in black,
    yellow, green, and
    purple; pencil
Scissors
Thick white crafts glue
Black tube-style paint

HERE'S HOW

1 Paint the entire pot
black and let it dry.
Choose a color to paint
the band around the top
of the pot. Let it dry. Make
white dots on the rest of
the pot by dipping the tip
of the paintbrush handle in
white paint and dotting it
onto the pot.

2 Use an appropriate
size dish, cup, or lid to
trace and cut a circle from
black foam about ½ inch
wider all around than the
pot opening. Place a small
amount of glue on the rim
of the pot. Press it on the
black foam circle.

3 To make the buckle,
measure the width of the
band of the pot (the part
painted a different color).

Cut a rectangle out of
foam about ⅛ inch higher
than the band on the pot.
Glue it to the band. Let
the glue dry.

4 Use a black tube-style
paint to write the guest's
name on the painted
band. Let it dry before
you use it.

131

evergreen greetings

Send holiday greetings in these quick-to-cut cards that the whole family will enjoy making.

Use this tree pattern to make cards, gift tags, tree ornaments, or gift bag trims!

TREE PATTERN

YOU'LL NEED

Colored paper in blue, red, yellow, green, purple, white, or other colors

Ruler

Pencil

Scissors

Glue stick

Tracing paper

Large paper punch

GOOD IDEA

Glue sequins or small buttons on the trees to decorate them for the holidays!

HERE'S HOW

1 Measure and cut the background paper to 5×10 inches. Fold the short ends together. Cut the next border piece 4¼×4¼ inches. Glue it in the center of the card front. Cut the tree background piece 4×4 inches. Glue it to the center of the card. Cut a white strip 3⅞×1 inch. Cut scallops along one long edge for snow. Glue the strip at the bottom of the center square, leaving a hint of border color.

2 Trace the tree pattern, *above*, onto tracing paper and cut it out. Trace around the pattern on green paper and cut it out. Glue the tree on a piece of white paper. Trim the white paper close to the tree, cutting a soft wavy line. Glue the tree in the center of the card.

3 Punch several circles from white paper. Glue the tiny white circles on the card to look like falling snow.

133

fingerprint gift tags

Roll up your
sleeves and
get ready for
some finger-
printing fun!

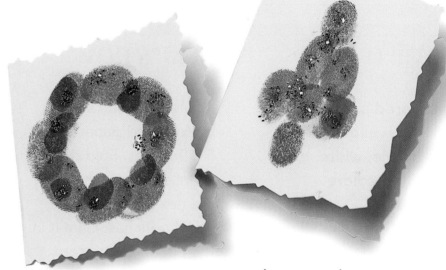

YOU'LL NEED

Assorted paper
Decorative-edge scissors,
   optional
Ink pads
Glitter glue

HERE'S HOW

1 Cut out or tear small
pieces of paper to use
as gift tags. If you wish,
trim the edges with
decorative-edge scissors.

2 Press a fingertip on an
ink pad, then on the tags.
Make holiday designs,
such as wreaths,
snowmen, and trees. Let
the ink dry.

3 To add sparkle, apply
glitter glue over the
design. Let the glue dry.

lasting

Capture the symbols of the seasons with these foam-print cards!

impressions

YOU'LL NEED

Clean foam food tray, such as Styrofoam
Dull pencil
Washable paint
Paintbrush
Heavyweight paper

HERE'S HOW

1 Use a dull pencil to draw a picture in the bottom of a clean foam tray.

2 Brush washable paint over the drawing in the tray.

3 Lay a piece of paper over the painted area. Gently press the paper down. Peel up the paper and let the paint dry.

GOOD IDEA
Glue three card fronts (in a row) to a large strip of colored cardboard and hang it on the wall!

seed bead bells

If you love to string beads, these ready-to-jingle bells are a joy to make.

YOU'LL NEED

Beading wire
Wire cutters
Seed beads
Ruler
2 jingle bells
Green ribbon
Cord or narrow ribbon
   for hanging

HERE'S HOW

1 Thread a 2-foot length of wire with seed beads. Form the length of the beaded wire into a bell shape by bending it back and forth in about 14 rows. The first row should be about 1½ inches wide.

The following rows should get wider until the last row is 3 inches.

2 Cut two lengths of wire, each 6 inches long. Thread the wire down through the end bead of each row. Use one wire for each side of the bell.

These two wires will hold the bell together. Thread the jingle bells onto a 3-inch length of wire and twist them to the bottom middle of the bell.

3 Loop a hanging cord through the top of the bell and tie a green ribbon bow on the hanging cord.

beaded wreath ornament

Use bracelet wire to make your wrists or your Christmas tree sparkle with beads!

YOU'LL NEED

Spring bracelet wire
Wire cutters
Needle-nose pliers
Glass beads
⅛-inch-wide gold ribbon
Gold cord for hanging

HERE'S HOW

1 Cut the spring wire into individual sections of 2½ coils each. Fold over the end of the wire with the needle-nose pliers.

2 Thread the whole length of wire with beads. Fold over the end with the pliers. To make an ornament, tie a ribbon bow on one side of the bracelet and a hanging cord from the other side.

merry greeting cards

These clever cards use techniques that will inspire card creation all year long.

YOU'LL NEED

Dark red matte card
  stock; paper plate
Acrylic paint in bright
  orange, deep red,
  and black; newspapers
Sponge paint roller;
  water
Plastic canvas

Gold paper; scissors
Decorative-edge scissors
Glue stick
Bright gold paint pen

HERE'S HOW

1 Experiment with different colors of paper

and paint. The paper used for this card is dark red and the paints are bright orange (much brighter than the paper), deep red (much darker than the paper), and black.

2 Cover the work area with newspapers. Spread

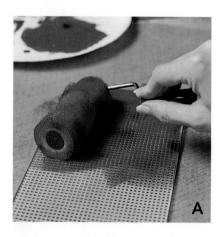

A

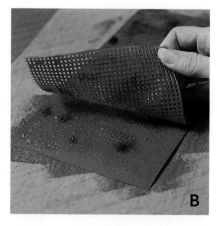

B

C

paint on a plate in three separate areas. Soak a sponge roller with water and squeeze out excess water. Use the wet roller to apply the paint.

3 Lay a piece of plastic canvas on the paper to be painted. Roll the damp roller into the paint, picking up some of all the colors but very little black as shown in Photo A,

opposite. Paint in random strokes over the plastic canvas. Use a generous amount of paint and repaint over areas if needed. Lift the plastic canvas occasionally to check the coverage, as shown in Photo B. Let the paint dry.

4 Cut the painted paper into shapes such as the star in the photo *above*.

You can glue the shape on coordinating paper to create a border and show-through cutout. Use decorative scissors to cut the edges if you want.

5 Use a gold paint pen to make designs or write words on the card, as shown in Photo C.

dancing snowmen jars

There's no men like snowmen, especially when they playfully watch over your sweet treats.

YOU'LL NEED

Glass jars
White air-dry clay, such as Crayola Model Magic
Metallic-color crafting wire
Wire cutters
Ice pick
Metallic-color beads
Clear adhesive, such as E6000
Acrylic enamel paint in black and white
Toothpicks
White glass paint
Pencil with round-tip eraser
Ribbon

HERE'S HOW

1 Wash the jar. Let it dry. Do not touch the areas to be decorated.

2 Shape three small balls from clay for each snowman. Press the balls together. Lay the jar on its side. Place a snowman on the jar and press it gently against glass.

3 Cut and shape wire arms, nose, and hat, if you want. To make a small cone nose, ask a grown-up to wrap wire around the end of an ice pick. While the clay is still moist, push the wire pieces in place and turn each slightly to make sure it is secure. Push in beads for buttons. Let the clay dry on the jars.

4 Remove the clay shapes from the jar. Glue them to the jar. Let the glue dry.

5 Dip a toothpick in paint to dot on eyes and a mouth.

6 If you want, add polka dots to a candy jar lid. Dip the eraser end of a pencil in white glass paint and dot it on the surface. Let the paint dry.

7 Tie a ribbon bow around the jar top. Trim the ribbon ends.

stacking
santas

As adorable as stacking toys, this trio will bring lots of ho-ho-hos to your holidays.

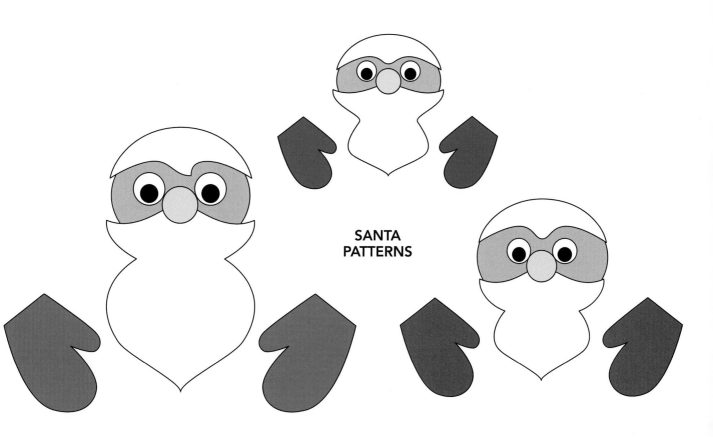

SANTA PATTERNS

YOU'LL NEED

Dinner- and snack-size
    paper plates in
    holiday colors
Scissors; stapler
Tracing paper; pencil
White felt
Colored paper
Wiggle eyes, pom-poms,
    button or other trims
Thick white crafts glue
Embroidery floss in
    red or green

HERE'S HOW

1 Cut the paper plate in half. Overlap the cut ends and staple them together.

2 Trace the patterns, *above*, onto tracing paper

GOOD IDEA
Tie these St. Nicks to holiday gifts, on a wreath, or hang them from stocking hangers on the mantel.

and cut them out. Use the patterns to cut face details and mittens from paper or felt.

3 Look at the photo, *opposite*, for ideas, and glue on the pieces and trims. Let the glue dry. Cut a 6-inch-long piece of embroidery floss. Knot the ends. Push a loop though a hole at the top of each santa for a hanger.

sparkling cone trees

Made from crepe
paper, you won't
have to pick up
needles from these
holiday trees.

GOOD IDEA

Ask mom for old pierced earrings, they make great trims for your tree!

YOU'LL NEED

Foam cones, such as Styrofoam
Crepe paper streamer in shades of green
Gold-head pins or straight pins
Gold beads
Gold star sequins
Narrow pipe cleaners

HERE'S HOW

1 Start at the bottom of the foam cone and wrap crepe paper streamer up around the cone, overlapping the layers to cover all the cone. Push a pin into the top of the cone to hold the crepe paper end.

2 To decorate the tree, thread a gold bead, then a star sequin onto a gold pin. Push the pin into the crepe-covered cone. Add trims until the tree is decorated how you like it.

3 Thread three gold beads onto a pipe cleaner. Fold the pipe cleaner and thread on three more beads to make one star point. Keep doing this until you make five beaded star points. Twist the pipe cleaner ends together to form a star. Push the pipe cleaner end into the top of the cone.

wooden menorahs

Light up the season with these colorful candleholders.

YOU'LL NEED

Wood beads, wheels,
  and spools
Acrylic paint in colors
  you like
Paintbrush
Pipe cleaners
Thick white crafts glue
Fabric paint pens
Birthday candles
Plastic birthday cake
  candleholders
Small metal washers

HERE'S HOW

1 Paint the wood pieces solid colors as you like. Let them dry.

2 To make a candlestick, double a pipe cleaner and cover it with glue. Slip several painted wood pieces onto the pipe cleaner. Let the glue dry. Decorate the candlesticks with paint pens, as you wish. Slip a candle into a plastic candleholder and slide the holder through a metal washer and into the hole of the top bead of the candlestick.

GOOD IDEA
Always ask a grown-up to light candles and to watch them while they are burning.

147

happy

Celebrate the new year with pop-open party favors that are full of surprises.

new year
crackers

YOU'LL NEED

Paper towel tubes
Scissors; ruler
Wrapping paper
Tape
Curling ribbon
Small candies

HERE'S HOW

1 Make sure the paper towel tube is clean inside and out. Ask a grown-up to cut tubes about 6 inches long, then cut each tube in half.

2 Cut a piece of wrapping paper 11×6 inches. Center the tubes end to end on the paper, leaving a 1-inch space between the tubes. Wrap paper around the tubes and tape the ends of the paper.

3 Tie one end of the paper with curling ribbon. Fill the open end with candy. Tie the end shut. Use scissors to curl the ends of the ribbon.

4 Have family or friends break the tubes in half to find the candy inside.

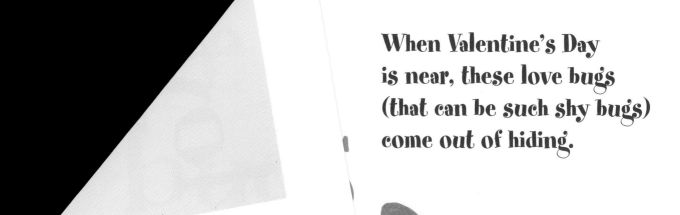

When Valentine's Day
is near, these love bugs
(that can be such shy bugs)
come out of hiding.

YOU'LL NEED

Wood hearts
Paint or markers
Scissors; sequins
**Paper, felt, and crafting
  foam scraps**
Wiggle eyes
Small feathers; pom-poms
Thick white crafts glue
**Adhesive-backed
  jewelry pins**

HERE'S HOW

1 Color hearts with paint or markers. Let them dry.

2 From scraps, cut out and glue spots and wings to the heart body. Glue on wiggle eyes. Glue paper legs to the underside and bend at the knees. Cut and glue on antennae. Decorate with trims. Let the glue dry.

3 Attach the pin to the bottom of the bug.

hearty bouquet

Go ahead–shower everyone with love with this endearing heart bouquet.

YOU'LL NEED

White and red air-dry clay, such as Crayola Model Magic
Green pencils
Green crafting foam scraps
Scissors; ribbon
Green pipe cleaners

HERE'S HOW

1 With your fingers, mix three parts white with one part red clay. If you need help, ask a grown-up.

2 For each heart roll out a 1-inch ball and make a dent in the top for the top of the heart.

3 Push the pencil eraser into the bottom of the ball. Flatten and smooth the clay toward the top of the ball to form two rounded heart tops.

4 Roll out a small coil of white clay and shape into a heart. Lightly press the coil on the pink heart. Let the hearts air-dry overnight.

5 Cut leaf shapes from crafting foam. Poke the end of a pipe cleaner through the leaf. Fold the pipe cleaner over to hold the leaf in place and twist it around the pencil. Tie the bouquet with ribbon.

151

Sweet cards

With a little cutting and pasting, you can make special Valentine cards with your message inside.

YOU'LL NEED

Construction paper
Ruler; marking pens
Scissors; white glue
Sucker, tea bag, and
**   heart-shape balloon**
Transparent tape

HERE'S HOW

1 For each card, cut a 7½×10 inch piece of construction paper. Fold it in half.

2 For the sucker card, cut out a red and white heart and glue them to the card. Cut out two green leaves, draw veins, and glue them on. Make a loop of transparent tape and attach the sucker to the card. Inside the card, write: For my sweetheart.

3 For the tea bag card, draw a tea cup, decorate it with marking pens, cut it out, and glue it to the card. Attach tea bag with a loop of transparent tape. Inside the card, write: You're my cup of tea.

4 For the balloon card, cut out a yellow sun and white clouds. Glue them on the card. Attach the balloon with a loop of transparent tape. Inside the card, write: Valentine, you blow me away.

candy from Cupid

for Sam from Ann XO

GOOD IDEA

Tape a wrapped piece of candy to the arrow for an added sweet treat.

With sweet treats accompanying sweet sentiments, these valentine greetings are a double gift from YOU!

YOU'LL NEED

Colored paper; pencil
Scissors; marking pens
Paper punch
Flavor straw, such as
   Pixy Stix
Colored feathers; tape

HERE'S HOW

1 Trace and cut out a heart from pink paper. See *pages 158–159* for several heart patterns.

2 Write a message in the center of the heart with a marking pen.

3 Punch a hole in the top of one side of the heart. Make another hole near the bottom of the heart.

4 Poke the flavor straw through the holes. Make sure it goes behind your message.

5 Tape two feathers to the top of the flavor straw.

6 Cut out a small paper heart and tape it to the bottom of the flavor straw.

153

blooming hearts

Send a flowerpot full of "I love yous" with these cute paper-heart blooms.

Trace these patterns to make a flowerpot full of love!

LEAF HEART PATTERN

FLOWER HEART PATTERN

YOU'LL NEED

Tracing paper; pencil
Scissors
Paper in pink, purple, green, and red
Black marking pen
Paper fastener
Straws
Flowerpot; acrylic paint and brush, optional
Foam ball, such as Styrofoam
Candy conversation hearts
Ribbon

HERE'S HOW

1 Trace the heart patterns, *above*. Cut them out. Use the patterns to cut large red, pink, and purple paper hearts for flowers and small green hearts for leaves. Write messages on the large hearts as you wish.

2 Stack three or four large hearts together. Pierce a paper fastener through the bottom of the hearts and into the top of a straw. Do the same for the leaves as shown in the photo, *opposite*.

3 Paint the flowerpot, if you want to, and let it dry. Wedge a foam ball into the flowerpot. Stick the straws into the foam. Fill the flowerpot with candy hearts. Tie a ribbon bow around the pot.

155

heart print cards

Made from your handprints, these cards will send happy messages.

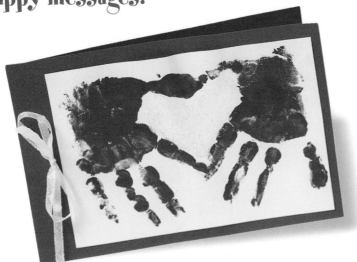

YOU'LL NEED

Acrylic paint in red
  and white
Card stock in red
  and white
Red and opalescent
  glitter glue, optional
Paper plate
Paintbrush
Paper in red and white
Ribbons
Paper punch
Scissors
Glue stick

HERE'S HOW

1 **To make the handprint heart,** *above left,* ask a grown-up to brush paint over your palm and fingers. Print one hand; apply paint to the other hand and line it up with the printed thumb and first finger so the space between your hands makes a heart. Brush a little glitter glue over the paint.

2 **To make the heart,** *above right,* squeeze out paint onto a paper plate and ask a grown-up to brush it on the outside of your hand along the pinky and palm. Curl your pinky to form the top of the heart. Have a grown-up help push your hand onto the red paper to print half the heart. Do the same thing with your other hand for the other half of the heart.

3 Cut out the heart prints. Glue them on folded card stock. Punch two holes on the sides and tie a ribbon through the holes.

beaded valentines

Even if you're a first-time stitcher, you can make these adorable cards with embroidery floss, beads, and felt.

YOU'LL NEED

Letter beads
Embroidery floss; needle
Scissors
Decorative-edge scissors
Felt in colors you like
Tracing paper; pencil
Thick white crafts glue
Card stock; envelopes
Metallic marking pens in
  gold and silver

HEART PATTERN

HERE'S HOW

1 Decide what words you would like to put on the card. Find those beads.

2 Thread the needle with three plies of embroidery floss. Sew beads on the felt with about 2 inches on each side.

3 Cut the felt with regular or decorative-edge scissors into a rectangle, heart, or other shape. For heart patterns, see the pattern *left* or on pages 158–159. Trace the pattern onto tracing paper and cut it out. If you want, cut a second felt shape a little bigger than the first. Glue the shapes together.

4 Cut and fold the card stock to the size you want to make the card. Glue the felt shape in the center. Let the glue dry.

5 Draw straight or dotted line borders with the metallic marking pens.

HEART PATTERNS

hugs 'n' Kisses
necKlace

Tell friends how special
they are with a necklace filled
with hugs and kisses.

160

YOU'LL NEED

Nylon beading thread
Beading needle
Large seed beads in
  white and red
Yardstick; scissors

HERE'S HOW

1 Without cutting the thread from the spool, thread on groups of eight beads, alternating red and white. String on beads until there are 15 groups of each color. Knot the thread ends, leaving one 36-inch tail of thread. Trim the thread.

2 With 36-inch thread in needle, push the needle through several inches of beads and push the needle out after two white beads, as shown in Diagram A, *right*.

3 To make an X, work left to right. Thread seven red beads onto the needle, as shown in Diagram B. Push the beads close to the necklace. Skip the last bead and push the needle

back through three beads as shown in Diagram C. Add three more red beads, as shown in Diagram D. Skip the last bead and push the needle back through two beads and through the center bead. Add three more red beads. Attach them to the necklace by pushing the needle through two white necklace beads, as shown in Diagram E, and the next four red beads.

4 To make an O, thread 12 white beads on the needle as shown in Diagram F. Push the beads close to the necklace. Push the needle through the first white bead, then through the four red beads and two white beads on the necklace, as shown in Diagram G.

5 Make four red Xs and three white Os. Run the thread through the necklace beads until the thread ends can be knotted together. To hide the thread ends, weave it into beads in both directions. Trim the thread ends.

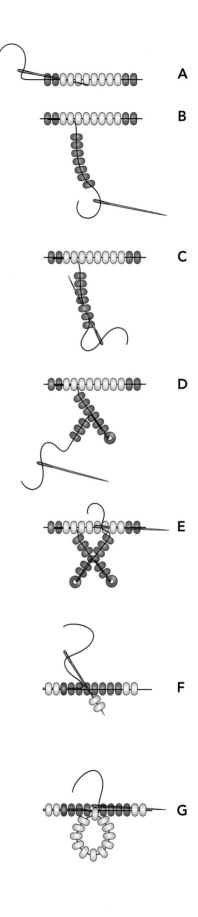

A

B

C

D

E

F

G

bloomin' egg family

Now here's a funny and fragile family you can make with egg faces and plants for the hair!

YOU'LL NEED

3 eggs
Paring knife or sharp
   pointed object
Bowl
1¼-inch-diameter
   wrapping paper tube
Ruler
Scissors, including
   decorative-edge
   scissors
Construction paper in
   yellow, turquoise, blue,
   black, white, and
   orange
Thick white crafts glue
Tracing paper

Pencil
3½-inch-long strand of
   pearl beads
Two ½-inch-diameter
   buttons
Black ultra-fine-point
   permanent marking
   pen; red marking pen
Tiny plants

GOOD IDEA
Be sure to wash
your hands often
when working
with eggs.

HERE'S HOW

1 Wash the eggs in warm
soapy water, rinse, and let
them dry. Ask an adult to
poke a hole in the narrow
end of each egg with a
knife or pointed object.

2 Enlarge the hole until
a finger will fit through.

3 Use your fingers to
carefully pinch off small
pieces of shell around the
hole, making it a little
bigger than a quarter.

continued on page 164

163

bloomin' egg family

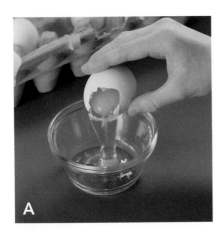

A

B

Pour out the egg as shown in Photo A. Rinse the shells. Set them aside to dry.

4 Cut the paper tube into a 2-inch-long tube for the father and 1⅝-inch-long tubes for the mother and the child.

5 Cut a 2×4¼-inch black paper rectangle for the father, a 1⅝×4¼-inch turquoise paper for the mother, and a 1⅝×4¼-inch yellow paper for the child. Wrap the paper around the tube and glue the overlapping edges together, as shown in Photo B.

6 Trace the father's bow tie and collar from the patterns, *opposite*, onto tracing paper and cut them out. Trace the collar pattern onto white paper and the bow tie onto orange paper. Cut them out. Glue the collar around the black tube just below the top edge. Glue the bow tie to the front.

7 Cut a ½×4¼-inch strip of yellow paper. Trim one long edge with the decorative-edge scissors to make a scallop collar. Glue the collar around the top edge of the turquoise tube. Glue the beads to the turquoise tube at the top edge to look like a necklace.

8 Cut three ⅛×4¼-inch strips of blue paper. Glue them around the yellow tube to make stripes. Glue the buttons down the front.

9 Look at the face patterns, *below*, and draw each of the faces on an egg with a pencil (the open end will be at the top).

10 Go over the pencil lines using a black marking pen as shown in Photo C. Make the lips and cheeks using the red marking pen.

11 Glue each of the eggs to its decorated tube. Fill the decorated eggs with dirt and plant tiny plants inside.

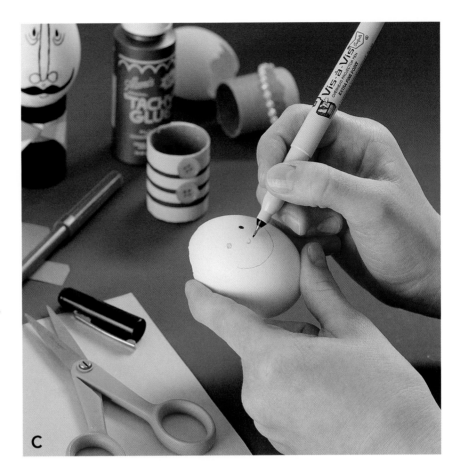

C

MOTHER

These patterns are for your egg family.

CHILD

FATHER'S BOW TIE

FATHER

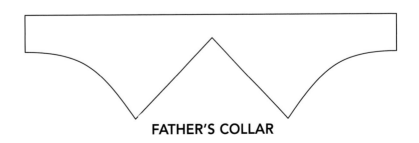

FATHER'S COLLAR

165

stars and stripes eggs

Decorate eggs with star stickers and rubber bands before you dye them in pretty pastel colors.

YOU'LL NEED

Hard-boiled or
  blown-out eggs
Commercial egg dye
  or food coloring
Star stickers
Rubber bands

HERE'S HOW

1 Ask a grown-up to make the egg dye as instructed on the package or use food coloring to dye the eggs.

2 To make the star eggs, press star stickers on the undyed eggs. Rub carefully around the edges of the stickers. Dip the eggs in the dye. Let the dye dry. Remove the stickers.

3 To make the striped eggs, wrap rubber bands around the eggs, using wide rubber bands or more than one size rubber band. Dip the eggs in the dye. Let the dye dry. Remove the rubber bands.

GOOD IDEA
Cover your eggs with round stickers to make polka dots.

"eggceptional" eggs

Gather pencils, a toothbrush, adhesive bandages, and toothpicks, and you're ready to decorate eggs!

YOU'LL NEED

Hard-boiled or blown-out
  eggs
Acrylic paint in any color
Paintbrush
Cardboard paper
  towel tube
Masking tape
Disposable plate
Toothbrush; toothpicks
Pencil with new eraser
Adhesive bandages
Scissors

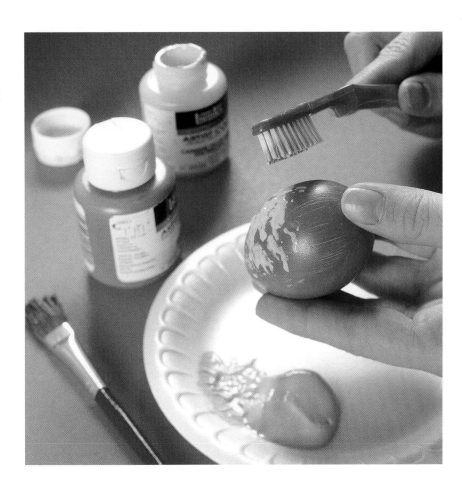

HERE'S HOW

1 If you want the background color to be white or brown, just decorate a plain egg. For other colors, paint the egg a solid color and let it dry. To keep the egg from rolling, cut a short section from a paper towel tube and tape it to the table.

2 **For the toothbrush (marbleized) technique,** pour paint onto a plate. Dip the toothbrush bristles into the paint and dot the egg as shown in the photo, *above*. Let one side dry, then paint the other side. Let it dry.

continued on page 170

169

"eggceptional" eggs

A

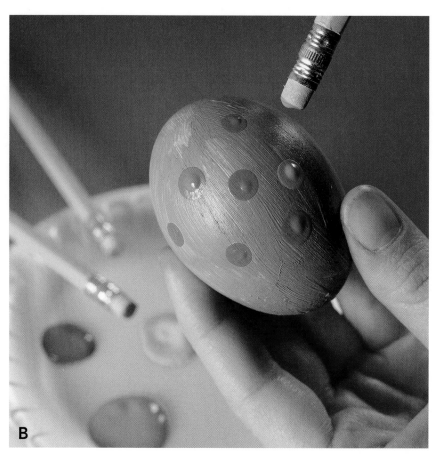

B

3 **For the toothpick (flower) technique,** choose two colors of paint to decorate your egg and pour those paints on the disposable plate. To make the petals of the flower, dip about ¼ inch of the toothpick into the paint; then lay the toothpick down on the egg to make a petal, as shown in Photo A. Make petals in a circle, as shown on the floral egg in the photo, leaving a space in the middle for the flower center. Work on one side of the egg at a time. Let the paint dry. Use a new toothpick and another color of paint. Dip just the tip of the toothpick in the paint and dot the center two or three times. Let the paint dry.

4 **For the pencil eraser (spotted) technique,** pour some paint onto a disposable plate. Dip the end of the eraser in the paint and dot the egg, as shown in Photo B. Paint the dots any color. Dot on one color at a time. Wash

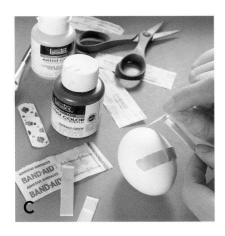

C

or wipe off the eraser before changing colors. Work on one side of the egg at a time. Let the paint dry.

5 For the adhesive bandages (striped) technique, leave the egg natural; do not paint it. Cut large bandages in half lengthwise or use small bandages to decorate the egg. Overlap the bandage strips, as shown in Photo C, or make whatever design you choose. Work

D

on one side of the egg at a time and paint the egg. Let the paint dry. Paint the other side, covering all of the bandages. Try to keep the paint from running underneath the bandage edges. Let the paint dry. Carefully peel off the bandages, as shown in Photo D. There will be

eggshell-color stripes when the bandages are peeled off.

egg flowers

Grow everlasting paper blooms in all the colors of spring.

GOOD IDEA

For flower centers you can display year-round, use small bouncy balls in bright colors.

YOU'LL NEED

Pencil
Cardboard tubes
Construction paper
Scissors
Thick white crafts glue
Rubber bands
Dyed or decorated
  Easter eggs

HERE'S HOW

1 Draw a flower on colored construction paper. Trace the tube end onto the middle of the flower.

2 Poke hole in center of circle. Create flaps for attaching flowers to tube by making small cuts from the center hole to the edge of the circle. Bend up flaps.

3 Glue flaps to outside of the tube. Glue green construction paper around tube, using rubber bands to secure until dry. Remove rubber bands. Cut leaves and glue to tube. Place a colored egg in the top of the tube.

egg rabbit

Create Easter bunny friends to play with and make you smile!

YOU'LL NEED

Tracing paper; pencil
Scissors
Felt scraps
Foam egg, such
  as Styrofoam
Colored straight pins
Thick white crafts glue
Pom-poms; pipe cleaner
Ribbon

HERE'S HOW

1 Trace the patterns, *right,* onto tracing paper. Cut out the shapes. Trace around patterns on felt. Glue the felt pieces to egg.

2 Poke pins through both felt and foam egg for eyes. Add felt trim to ears.

3 Glue on pom-pom nose and tail. Cut two 2-inch-long pieces of pipe cleaner. Poke the pipe cleaners under the nose for whiskers. Tie a bow with ribbon and glue it under the neck.

GOOD IDEA
Place a bunny or two in an Easter basket with colorful eggs and use as a centerpiece!

HEAD PATTERN

FRONT LEG PATTERN

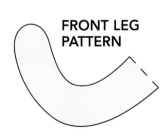

HIND LEG PATTERN

173

glittery eggs

To make elegant eggs,
paint on a glaze of glitter
fingernail polish and trim them
with tiny metallic beads.

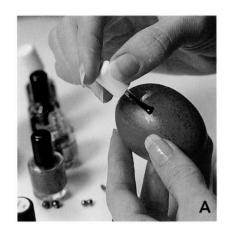

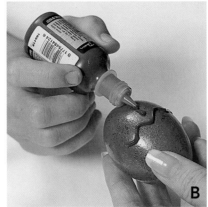

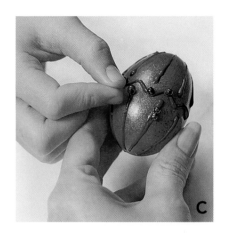

YOU'LL NEED

Plaster or wood eggs
Bright color
  acrylic paint
Paintbrush
Assorted glitter
  nail polish
Fabric paint pen
Small glass or
  metallic beads
Pretty bowl

HERE'S HOW

1 Paint the eggs with acrylic paint. Let the paint dry. Apply a second coat if needed. Let the paint dry.

2 To add glitter apply nail polish on the eggs, as shown in Photo A, *above left.* Try different color combinations. On these eggs, green, aqua, purple, and pink nail polishes were used on the magenta egg; lime green and aqua polishes were used on the green egg; orange and pink polishes were used on the yellow egg. Let the nail polish dry.

3 Decorate the egg however you want with fabric paint, as shown in Photo B. Add swirls, lines, zigzags, or any other shapes to one side at a time. Place beads in the wet paint, as shown in Photo C. Let the paint dry. Turn the egg over and decorate the other side. Let the paint dry.

4 Arrange the eggs in a bowl.

go outside and

ladybugs, stick frames, and glasses for sun—this outdoor chapter is loaded with fun! You'll make garden stakes, bug boxes, and seed decanters—not to mention, watering-can planters! These outside projects have lots of whistles and bells, when you use stuff like rocks and seashells!

find some FUN!

sturdy-as-a-rock
paperweight

Make your favorite
animal to use as a weight
to hold all your important
school papers.

YOU'LL NEED

Rocks

Strong adhesive, such
  as E6000

Acrylic paint in colors
  you like

Paintbrush

Glitter glue

Pipe cleaners

Scissors

Felt

HERE'S HOW

1 Arrange small rocks to look like a turtle, ladybug, or other critter you like. Glue the rocks together. Let the glue dry.

2 **For the ladybug,** paint the body red, the head black, and the eyes white. Let the paint dry. Paint a black line down the center of the body. Paint black dots on the eyes and on the body. Paint a white smile. Use glitter glue to make circles around the black dots on the body. Let the paint dry.

3 **For the turtle,** paint the body green, the head and feet brown, the nose red, and the eyes white. Let the paint dry. Paint

GOOD IDEA

Use large rocks to make silly creatures to place in your garden or along a walkway.

brown dots on the body and on the top portion of the eyes. Paint black dots below the eyelids. Paint a black smile and black toes on the feet. Use glitter glue to draw between the circles on the body. Let the paint dry.

4 If you want, make antennae by twisting a pipe cleaner around the ladybug neck; twist the ends.

5 Cut a piece of felt to fit the bottom of the paperweight. Glue it on the bottom. Let the glue dry.

funky Sunglasses

Dress up a pair of sunglasses with tiny treasures to make a decorative fashion statement.

YOU'LL NEED

Child's plastic sunglasses
Paint pens in colors
    you like, optional
Assorted small objects,
    such as animals,
    seashells, or erasers
Quick-grab epoxy

HERE'S HOW

1 If you want to draw designs on your sunglasses, use the paint pens to make dots, squiggles, or stripes.

2 Plan how to arrange the assorted small objects on the glasses. You may place them on the frame around the lenses and toward the front of the bows. Avoid placing objects directly over the ear area.

3 Ask a grown-up to help you epoxy the objects one by one onto the sunglasses. You may need to hold each object in place for a minute until the glue sets.

stick-to-it easel

This stick frame is so neat—don't be surprised if mom or dad wants you to make one for their desk!

YOU'LL NEED

For the easel
4 sticks the same length, about 9 inches long
Thick white crafts glue
Embroidery floss
For the framed picture
Your drawing or painting glued to cardboard
8 sticks about the same length to fit around the picture
Pliers or wire-cutter tool
Thick white crafts glue
Embroidery floss

182

HERE'S HOW

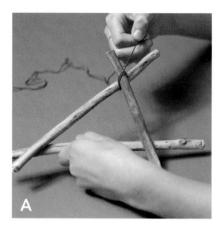

A

For the easel

1 Make an "A" with three sticks. Use a little bit of glue to hold them together. Let the sticks set until they stay together. Carefully pick up the sticks and add more glue at the two bottom corners. Wrap the floss around and around the wet glue, as shown in Photo A, *above*.

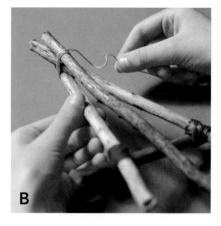

B

2 When the two bottom corners are wrapped, add a little bit of glue to the back stick and place it against the first two. Hold it together and wrap floss around the top of all three sticks as shown in Photo B.

For the frame

1 If the drawing is not on cardboard, cut it out and glue it to a piece of cardboard.

2 Break off four straight sticks the same size as the edges of the cardboard. Have a grown-up help if you need to use pliers or a wire-cutter tool. Glue the sticks to the edges of the cardboard.

3 Break four more sticks to fit inside the sticks you glued to the drawing. Put a little glue along the middle of the stick and wrap the floss around it. You can put a spot of glue over that floss and wrap another color on top if you wish (see Photo C).

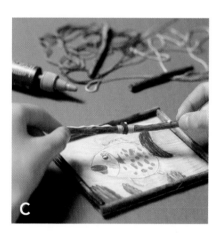

C

4 Glue the shorter sticks to the inside of the other sticks. Let the glue dry.

183

outdoor tic-tac-toe

Grab a friend and a shady spot to play this fun game that you can make in a flash.

YOU'LL NEED

Wood slice from a large
tree (found or
purchased)
Damp rag
Pencil or chalk
Small twigs
4 small pebbles
Thick white crafts glue
Clear gloss spray,
optional
2 different kinds of rocks
for markers—4 of each

HERE'S HOW

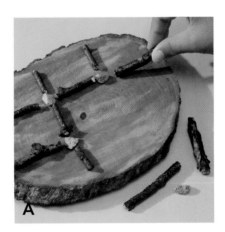

1 Clean the wood slice
with a damp rag. Use a
pencil or piece of chalk to
draw the tic-tac-toe grid
onto the wood, or break
the twigs and put them on
the wood as shown in
Photo A.

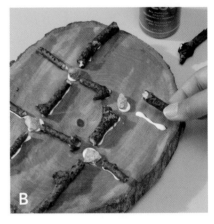

2 Glue the small
pebbles and the twigs to
the wood as shown in
Photo B. Let the glue dry.
If you wish, spray the top
with gloss spray.

3 Use the rocks
for markers.

GOOD IDEA
Use acorn caps
instead of small
pebbles between
the twigs.

stamp-it picnic tablecloth

Sponge colorful leaves around the edges of a tablecloth, then invite your best friends over for an outdoor tea party!

YOU'LL NEED

Tracing paper
Pencil
Scissors
Flat craft sponge
  (this is easy to cut and
  expands when you put
  it in water)
Dish and water to soak
  the sponge
Waxed paper
Acrylic paint or fabric
  paint
Foam plate
Purchased tablecloth

HERE'S HOW

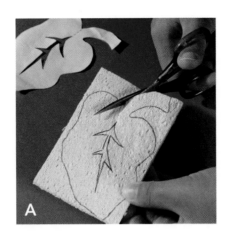

A

1 Lay tracing paper on the leaf pattern, *below*, and trace around the outlines and veins. Cut out the pattern. Trace the leaf onto the sponge and cut it out as shown in Photo A. To cut the leaf veins, fold the leaf tip to the stem. Cut the long vein. Open up the leaf and cut the shorter veins. Soak the sponge in water. Squeeze out the extra water.

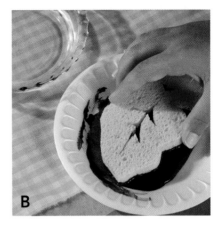

B

2 Cover your work surface with waxed paper. Put a small amount of paint on a foam plate. Dip one side of the sponge leaf into the paint and dab it once on the foam plate (see Photo B).

C

3 Stamp the leaf pattern around the edges of the tablecloth as shown in Photo C. Use the sponge two or three times before dipping it into the paint again. Let the paint dry.

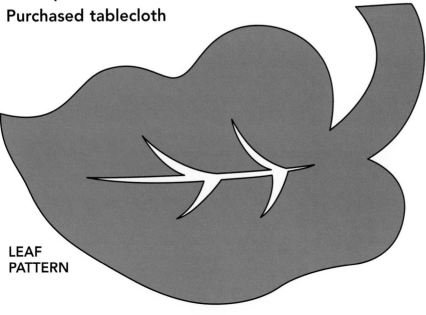

LEAF
PATTERN

creepy crawly bug box

Capture critters in a take-out box home of their own!

YOU'LL NEED

Paper grocery bag
Tracing paper; pencil
Scissors
12-inch-squares of
    card stock in light blue
    and white and scraps
    of yellow and red
Glue stick
Crafts knife
Scrap of polyfoam and
    heavy cardboard
Black and green ink pads
Leaf rubber stamp
Fixative spray
Green tube-style paint,
    such as Tulip Pearl 3-D
Black glass paint, such as
    Plaid Gallery Glass
Small wiggle eyes

Punches: ⅛-inch hole
    and swirl
Black mesh with an
    adhesive back
24-inch-long lengths of
    red and yellow
    18-gauge wire
Clear tape

HERE'S HOW

1 Ask a grown-up to help with this project. Cover your work surface with a paper grocery bag. Trace the box pattern on *pages 192–193* onto tracing paper. Cut out the pattern, including the diamond shapes. Glue the light blue card stock to the white card stock. Place the pattern on the white side of the layered cardstock

and draw around it. Cut out the box with scissors. Carefully cut out the diamonds and have a grown-up use a crafts knife to make a slit in the top flap.

2 Trace the ant pattern on *page 193* onto tracing paper. Cut out the pattern. Place the pattern on a piece of foam and draw around it. Cut out the ant. To make a stamp, glue the ant on a heavy piece of cardboard.

continued on page 190

189

creepy crawly bug box

A

B

3 Place the box shape blue side up on your work surface. Press the ant stamp in the black ink pad and stamp the ant on the box, as shown in Photo A. Ink the leaf stamp with green ink and stamp the leaf on the box. Let the ink dry. Spray the stamped side of the box with fixative.

4 Use 3-D paint to add dimension to the stamped leaves. Paint over the stems and make vein lines on each leaf.

5 Use black glass paint and squeeze a circle on each round section of the ant bodies (see Photo B). While the paint is wet, place two wiggle eyes in the paint on each ant head. Let the paint dry.

6 Punch swirls from red and yellow cardstock. Put glue on the backs of the swirls and press them onto the blue box.

7 Cut two pieces of mesh larger than the diamond openings. Press the sticky side of the mesh onto the white side of the box over the openings as shown in Photo C, *opposite.*

8 Fold the box into shape along the dashed lines. Glue the tabs to the box sides.

9 For the handle, wrap the wires around a pencil, leaving 1½ inches straight at the ends. Remove the pencil. Use the ⅛-inch hole punch to make two holes where marked on the pattern. Insert the handle ends into the holes. Tape down the wire ends inside the box. Stretch the handle so you can easily open the box.

10 Fold in the side flaps at the top of the box. Cut a mesh rectangle to fit the box top. Place the mesh over the side flaps. Close the top flaps.

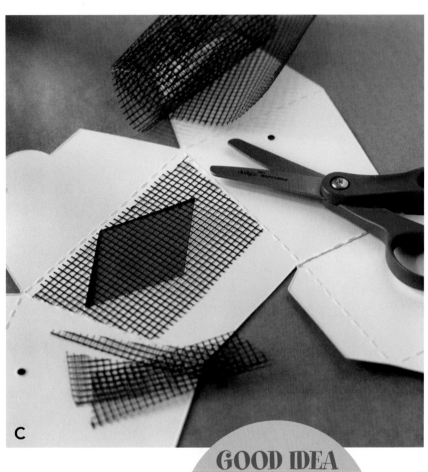

C

GOOD IDEA

Stamp the box with flowers, butterflies, or other designs and use it for a gift box!

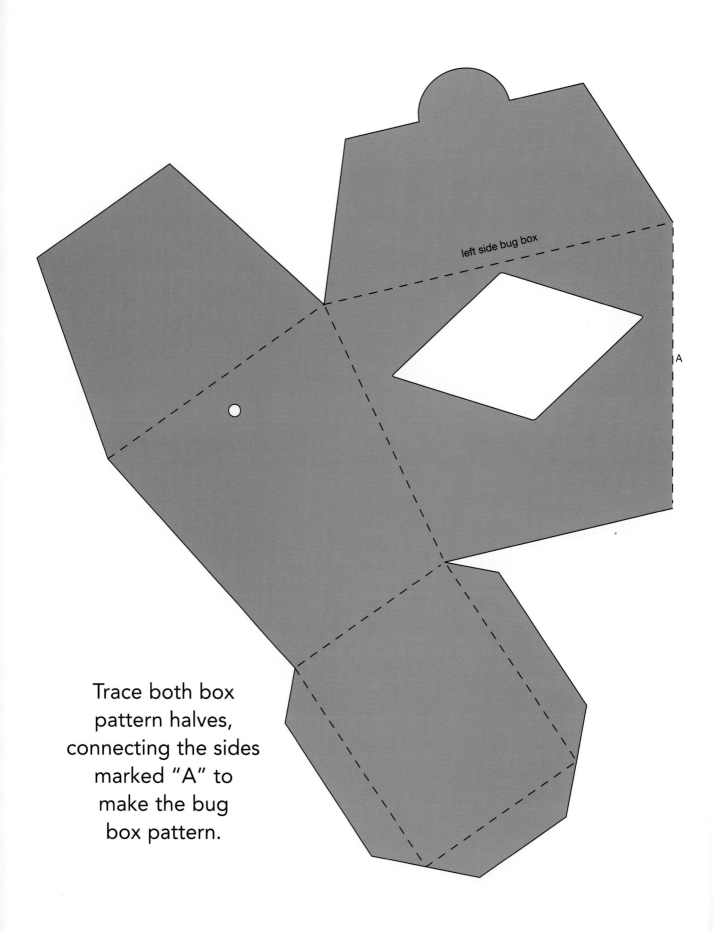

left side bug box

A

Trace both box
pattern halves,
connecting the sides
marked "A" to
make the bug
box pattern.

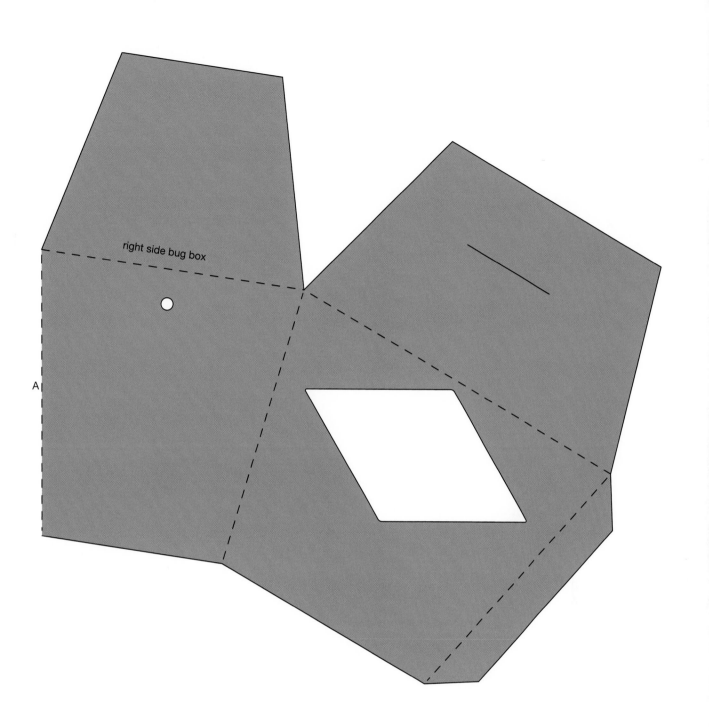

right side bug box

A

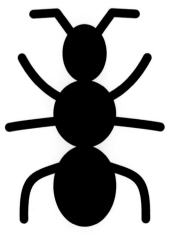

Trace this pattern to
make the ant stamp
for the bug box.

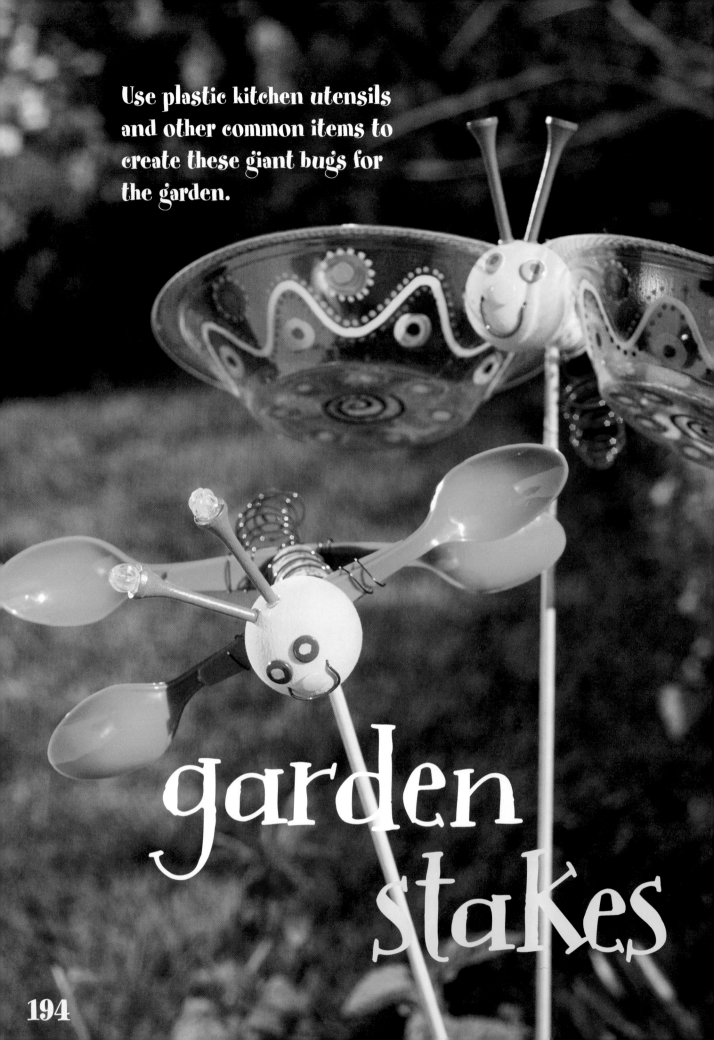

Use plastic kitchen utensils and other common items to create these giant bugs for the garden.

garden stakes

194

YOU'LL NEED

2 clear plastic bowls
Paint markers
Paper punch; ruler
22- and 24-gauge wire
  in colors you like
Wire cutters
1¾-inch-long cork
Colored wood golf tees
Foam practice golf ball
Plastic beads (optional)
Colored thumbtacks
Extra-tacky crafts glue
Pencil
¼-inch wooden dowel

HERE'S HOW

1 To make the wings, use the paint markers to decorate the outside of the clear plastic bowls. Punch two holes 1 inch apart on the rim of each bowl.

2 Ask a grown-up to cut two 18-inch lengths of 24-gauge wire. Line up the holes in the bowls and place the cork for a body between the bowls. Wrap one wire around the cork and through

a pair of holes several times to hold the wings in place. Wrap the second wire around the cork and through the other holes.

3 For the tail, cut a 24-inch length of 22-gauge wire. Coil the wire into a spiral. Wrap one end of the coiled wire around the cork and through the holes at the back of the body.

continued on page 196

195

butterfly garden stake

4 Use the pointed end of a golf tee to make two holes in the top of the foam ball. Glue the tees into the holes for the antennae. If you'd like, glue plastic beads to the top of the antennae.

5 Push thumbtacks into the front of the foam ball for the eyes and nose. Draw circles on the eyes with a paint marker. Shape a scrap of wire into a smile and bend back the ends at a right angle. Position the smile on the front of the ball and push the ends into the ball. Glue the head to the front of the cork body.

6 Use the point of a pencil to make a hole in the underside of the cork body. Glue one end of the dowel in the hole.

7 Push the opposite end of the dowel into the ground. Find the parts of the bowls that are lowest, and use a nail or other pointed object to punch a hole or two in each wing so the water will drain out.

dragonfly garden stake

YOU'LL NEED

The same last 10
  materials from the
  butterfly plant stake
  list, *page 195*
4 plastic spoons for
  the wings
Paint marker

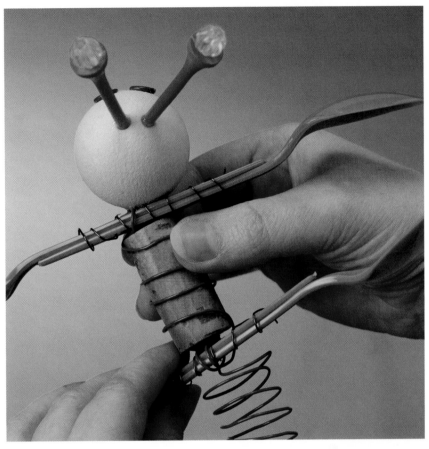

HERE'S HOW

1 For the wings, ask a
grown-up to cut two
8-inch lengths of 24-gauge
wire. Place two spoon
handles together with the
spoon bowls facing in the
opposite direction. Wrap
one piece of the wire
around the handles. Do
the same with the other
spoons and wire.

2 Cut a 24-inch length
of 22-gauge wire. Wrap
one end of the wire
around the cork body. Coil
the rest of the wire in a
spiral for the tail, as shown
in the photo, *above.*

3 Center and glue one
pair of wings on the front
of the cork body and the
second pair of wings on
the back, slipping the
wings in front of the tail.

4 Finish the dragonfly
following Steps 4, 5, and
6, *opposite.* Push the
opposite end of the dowel
into the ground.

197

Hang a set of glass lanterns in your garden. They're perfect for lighting the path at night.

firefly lights

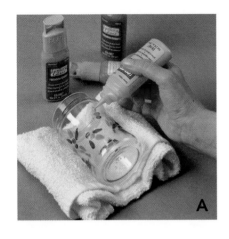

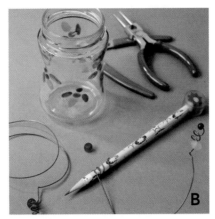

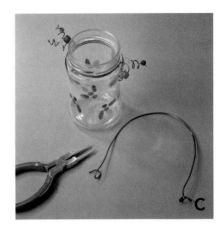

YOU'LL NEED

Waxed paper

Clean glass jar

Dish towel

Glass paint in colors
  you like

24-gauge colored wire
  in two colors

Wire cutters

Ruler

Pencil

Glass beads in
  assorted colors

Needle-nose pliers

Tealight candle

HERE'S HOW

1 Cover your work area with a sheet of waxed paper to protect it. Lay the jar on its side. To keep the jar from rolling, prop up the sides with a dish towel. Paint fireflies on the top half of the jar with glass paint as shown in Photo A, *above left*. Use the pattern, *below*, as a guide. Be careful not to squeeze out too much paint because it will drip down the sides of the jar. Let the paint dry.

2 Roll the jar over and paint the other side.

3 Ask a grown-up to help you cut two 24-inch-long pieces from one color of wire and an 18-inch-long piece from the second color of wire as shown in Photo B.

4 Wrap a 24-inch-long wire around the neck of the jar twice. Twist the ends together. To curl the wire, wrap the end around a pencil. Remove the pencil and thread glass beads onto the curls. Do the same for the second wire. Place the curls across from each other.

5 To make the handle, use needle-nose pliers to curl the ends of the 18-inch wire (see Photo C), then wrap them around the wrapped wire between the curls and the jar. Put a tealight candle in the jar. (Only a grown-up should light the candle.)

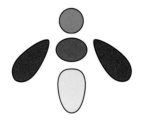

firefly pattern

199

Fill a jar with sand and shells from your beach vacation and give it to a friend.

beach in a jar

YOU'LL NEED

Glass jar with lid
Glass cleaner
Paint pen, optional
Sand
Shells, pebbles, small
    pieces of driftwood,
    and sea glass
Thick white crafts glue

HERE'S HOW

1 Use glass cleaner to remove fingerprints from the inside and outside of the jar.

2 Decide if the jar is going to sit on its bottom or lie on its side. If you like, use a paint pen to write the name of the place where you collected the shells on the side of the jar.

3 Pour enough sand into the jar to cover the bottom.

4 Drop shells, pebbles, pieces of driftwood, and sea glass inside the jar.

5 Glue a large shell, a sand dollar, or a group of shells on the lid. Let the glue dry. Put the lid on the jar.

see-through starts

Make indoor seed starters from plastic food containers decorated with handmade bugs.

YOU'LL NEED

Plastic berry or bakery
  boxes or egg carton,
  with the lids attached
Darning needle
Fine-tip paint markers
Small wiggle eyes
Brightly colored buttons
Thick white crafts glue
Colored paper clips
Potting soil
Seeds

HERE'S HOW

1 Decide where to put bugs on the lid and sides of your plastic container. Use the darning needle to poke two holes in the container for each bug and space the holes about ¼ inch apart. Use the paint markers to draw six legs radiating out from the pairs of holes.

2 Glue two wiggle eyes along the edge of each button as shown *above*. Be careful not to cover the holes in the buttons. Let the glue dry before you go to the next step.

3 Look at the photograph *opposite* for ideas. Use the paint markers to draw spots, stripes, or zigzags on the buttons.

4 To attach each button bug, unfold and straighten a colored paper clip, then fold the paper clip in half. Place a bug on the container over a pair of holes. From the inside of the container, thread the ends of the paper clip through the holes in the container and the button. Twist the ends of the

paper clip together to hold the button. Shape the ends into the antennae.

5 Make sure the bottom of the container has some drainage holes. If it doesn't, use scissors to poke a few holes. Put potting soil in the bottom of the container. Prepare the seeds following the instructions on the seed package. Plant the seeds, placing some along the edge of the container so you can see the roots grow. Water the soil, close the lid, and set the container on a plastic tray to avoid water damage. Place in a warm sunny spot. When the seeds sprout, open the lid. When the plants are large enough, transplant them into your garden.

leaf-it-to-nature frame

Take a nature walk and gather a handful of interesting leaves to make an out-of-this-world frame.

YOU'LL NEED

Leaves, clovers, ferns, or other flat fresh greenery
Picture frame and two mats
Scissors
Decoupage medium
Paintbrush
Picture or drawing

HERE'S HOW

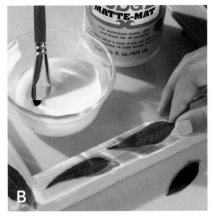

1 Decide how to arrange the greenery on the mats and frame as shown in Photo A, *above*. Trim the pieces if you need to.

2 Cover the front and sides of the frame with decoupage medium. Place the greenery on the frame, pressing the pieces into place (see Photo B).

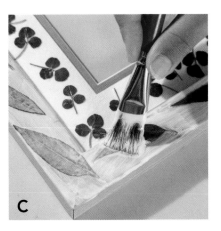

3 When all the pieces are arranged on the frame, add two more coats of decoupage medium, letting it dry between coats.

4 Decoupage greenery onto the mats the same way you did for the frame as shown in Photo C. Let all of the decoupage medium dry. Tape a drawing or photograph behind the mats and put the drawing into the frame.

GOOD IDEA
For a quicker, no-decoupage version of this framing idea, use stickers!

sculpt some FUN

Roll it, shape it, make it into a bead—clay can be baked or air-dryed, you'll see! Add that to beading and this chapter gets even better, you'll make dragonflies, necklaces, and frames with letters! Using clay and beads for these projects is fun, now to get started you have to pick one!

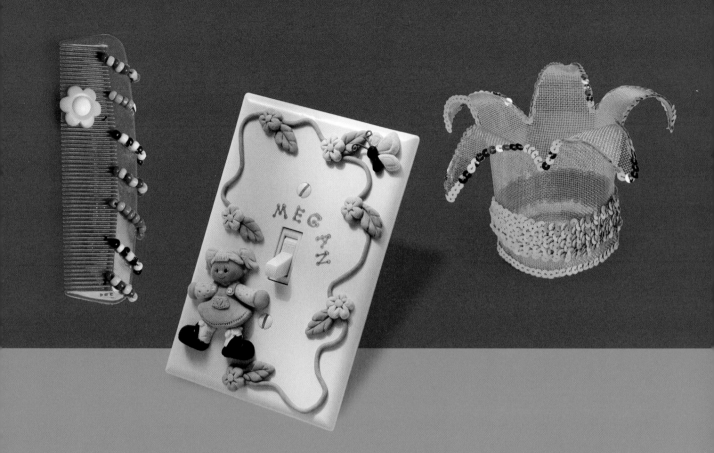

with clay and beads!

bouncy bead puppets

Adorable on a holiday tree or for you to play with, these smiling friends are made using beads.

YOU'LL NEED

Three 12-inch pieces of elastic string; scissors
9 wood beads: 2 for the hands, 2 for the feet, 2 for the body, 1 for the head and 2 for the hat
Miniature bell bead for hat
2 buttons
Permanent marking pen

HERE'S HOW

1 Cut three 12-inch-long pieces of string. Hold the pieces together and knot them 4 inches from one end. Cut off one piece close to the knot. The 2-strand end are the legs.

2 Use the diagram, *above right*, as a guide. For the feet, knot a bead onto the end of each of the two shorter string pieces.

3 For the body, pull the 3 strings through the two body beads.

4 For the hands, knot beads onto the end of 2 strings.

5 Thread the center string through the button, the head, another button, then the bell and round hat beads. Tie the string end into a loop.

6 Use a marking pen to draw a face on the bead between the buttons.

PUPPET DIAGRAM

Take-along pals fit easily into your pocket or purse and are ready to play at a moment's notice.

YOU'LL NEED

Tri-beads (available at crafts stores)
5-inch long pipe cleaner
16 mm wood bead
Paintbrush; acrylic paint or marking pens
Needle-nose pliers

bendable bead worms

HERE'S HOW

1 String the tri-beads onto the pipe cleaner. Add the wooden bead for the head.

2 Paint or draw on eyes and a mouth with paint or marking pens.

3 Use pliers to bend and twist the ends of the pipe cleaner toward the body.

Bend the body to look like a worm. If you make a loop at the bottom, the worm will be able to stand alone.

These beaded beauties will keep your hair in place when spring breezes blow.

dragonfly barrettes

YOU'LL NEED

Beading wire
Wire cutters
Ruler; a variety of glass
  beads including small
  beads for the wings
Barrette backs

HERE'S HOW

1 Fold a 16-inch piece of wire in half and thread a small bead onto the center fold of the wire. Thread four larger beads through both wire ends to make the dragonfly tail, as shown in Step 1, *below*.

Split the wires apart and thread 20 to 25 small beads onto each wire.

2 Fold the beaded section of wire in half to make a loop for the wing. Twist the loop at the base of the wing, as shown in Step 2.

3 Bring the wires back together and thread one or two large beads on both wires for the dragonfly body as shown in Step 3. Split the wires apart again and create a second pair of wings just like the first pair. Bring the wires together to thread on a large head bead.

Separate the wires to thread and twist a small eye bead on each wire. Spiral the remaining wire into antennae as shown in Step 4.

4 To attach the dragonfly to a barrette, lay it on the flat barrette back. Wrap a 3-inch wire over the neck and around the barrette a couple of times, then twist the wire ends together. Wrap another wire around the second to last tail bead to hold the other end of the bug on the barrette.

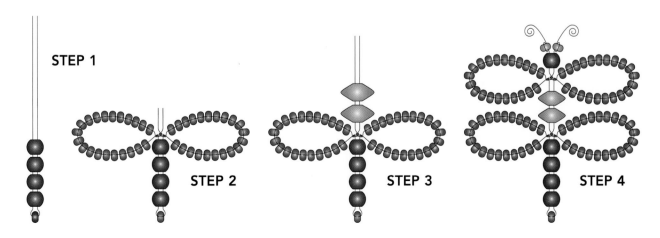

STEP 1   STEP 2   STEP 3   STEP 4

stone jewelry

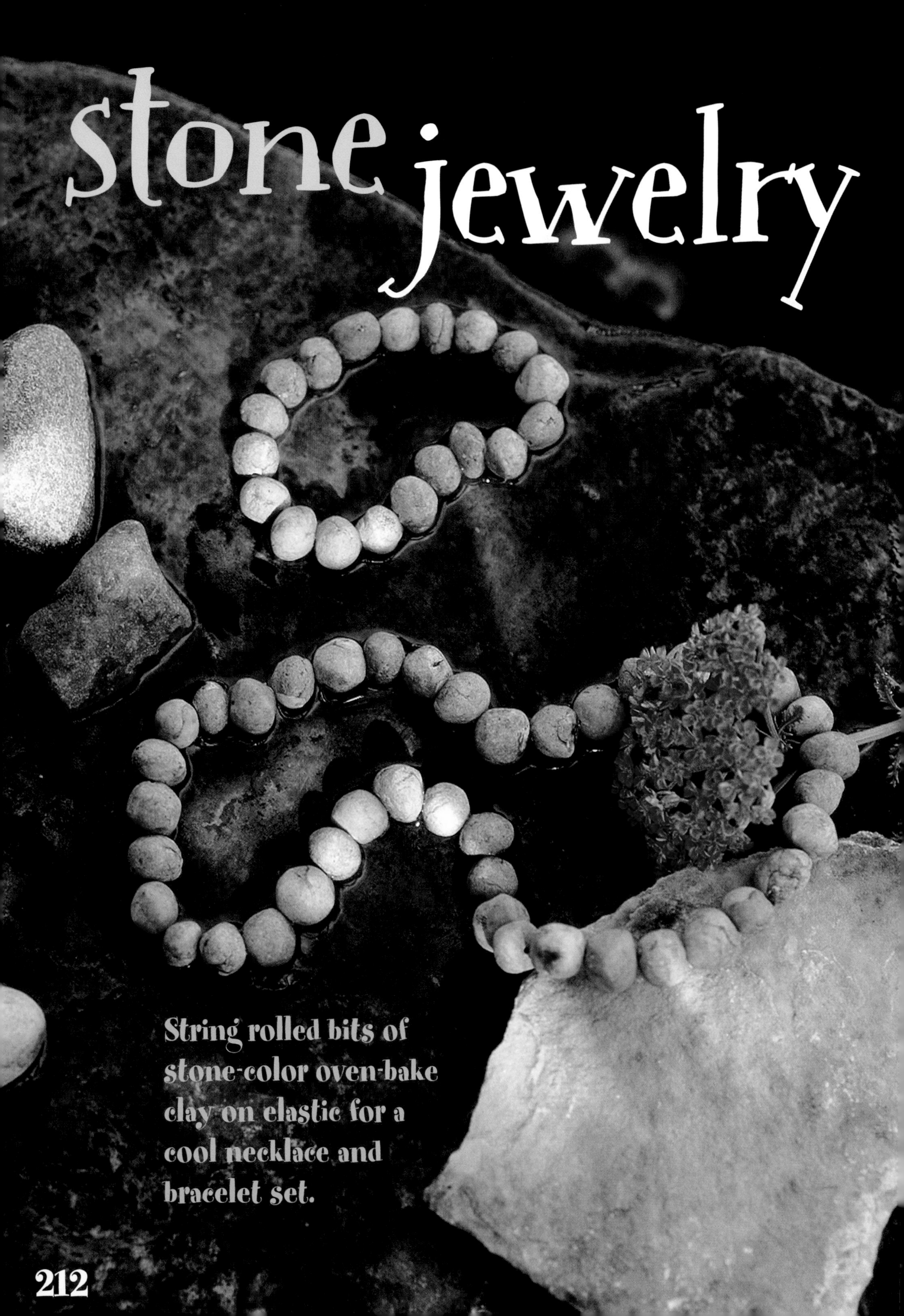

String rolled bits of
stone-color oven-bake
clay on elastic for a
cool necklace and
bracelet set.

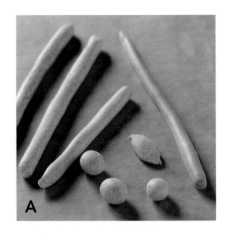
A

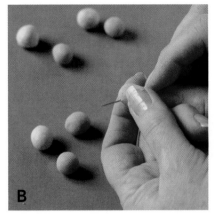
B

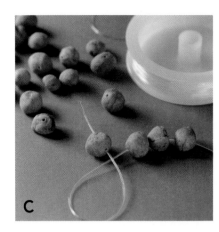
C

YOU'LL NEED

Waxed paper
Oven-bake clay, such as
**   Sculpey Granitex, in**
**   two colors**
Needle
Old file folder or
**   index cards**
Baking sheet
Old sock
Brown acrylic paint
Elastic thread for jewelry

HERE'S HOW

1 Cover your work area with a sheet of waxed paper. Roll about one fourth package of clay in your hands for a minute or two until it is soft and pliable. Roll the clay into a snake. Pinch off 30 pieces of clay all about the same size as shown in Photo A, *above*. Roll each piece into a ball about the size of a large pea. Make the balls irregular shapes to look like stones. Make a second color of clay stones.

2 To make a hole through each stone, twist a needle slowly through the clay balls (see Photo B).

3 Cover the baking sheet with an old file folder or index cards. Place the stones on the file folder and ask a grown-up to bake them in the oven according to the instructions on the clay package.

4 Squeeze a small amount of brown paint into the old sock. Place the baked stones in the sock and squish them around to cover the stones with paint.

5 Squeeze the stones out of the sock. Let the paint dry.

6 String the stones on the elastic as shown in Photo C. We used 40 stones for the necklace and 20 for the bracelet, but you can string on any number of beads that fits you. Knot the elastic ends together and trim the ends.

clay bead
rings

Create the center bead for each
of these colorful rings with simple
logs made of oven-bake clay.

GOOD IDEA
Instead of a rolling pin, use a smooth aluminum can to roll out your clay.

YOU'LL NEED

Polymer clays, such as
  Sculpey in 2 or 3 colors
Waxed paper
Ruler
Pencil or rolling pin
Sharp knife or crafts knife
Needle
Baking sheet covered
  with parchment paper
24-gauge beading wire
Wire cutters
Seed beads

HERE'S HOW

1 Look at the photo, *opposite*, and decide what colors you would like to use. Select two or three colors for the spiral beads. Use two, three, or four colors of clay for the flower-style beads.

2 Cover your work area with a sheet of waxed paper. Knead the clay in your hands for a minute or two until it is soft and pliable.

3 To make the clay beads, first make logs of clay and slice them.

4 To make a spiral log, flatten two or three colors of clay into very thin 2×6-inch sheets as shown in the Photo *above*. Use a pencil or rolling pin to flatten and stretch the clay on your work surface. Layer the sheets of clay and roll them into a log.

continued on page 216

215

clay bead rings

5 To make a flower log, roll one 6-inch-long thin snake for the flower center, four 6-inch-long thin snakes for the petals, and four 6-inch-long thin snakes for the background. Try to make all the snakes the same size. Place the flower petal snakes evenly around the flower center snake. Place the background snakes between the flower petals. Use a pencil or a rolling pin to flatten and stretch the clay into a thin sheet for the outside of the log. Wrap the clay sheet around the completed flower snakes as shown in Photo A, *right*.

6 Place the log in the refrigerator for a half-hour. Place the log on your work surface. Ask a grown-up to

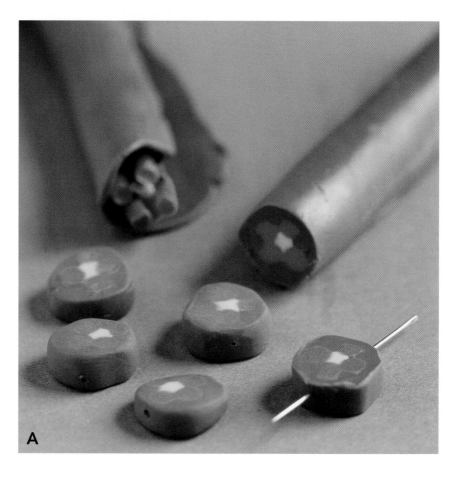

A

use a sharp knife or a crafts knife to slice ⅛- to ¼-inch-thick beads from the log, as shown in Photo B.

7 To make a hole through the beads, push a straight pin slowly through each bead from side to side as shown *above*. Be careful not to twist the design.

8 Place the beads on a baking sheet covered with baking parchment. Ask a grown-up to put the baking sheet in the oven and bake the beads according to the instructions on the package of clay.

B

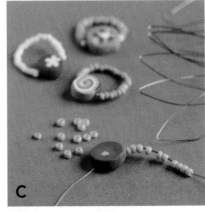

C

GOOD IDEA
Make bracelets for
your wrists and
ankles to match
your cool clay
rings!

9 Use wire cutters to cut a 6-inch length of beading wire for each ring. Thread enough seed beads on the wire to wrap around the back and sides of your finger.

10 Thread the cooled clay bead onto the wire (see Photo C). Check to be sure the ring fits your finger. Remove or add seed beads to fit the ring size. Thread the other end of the wire through the opposite side of the clay bead. Wrap the wire ends around the threading wire at each side of the clay bead. Trim off the excess wire.

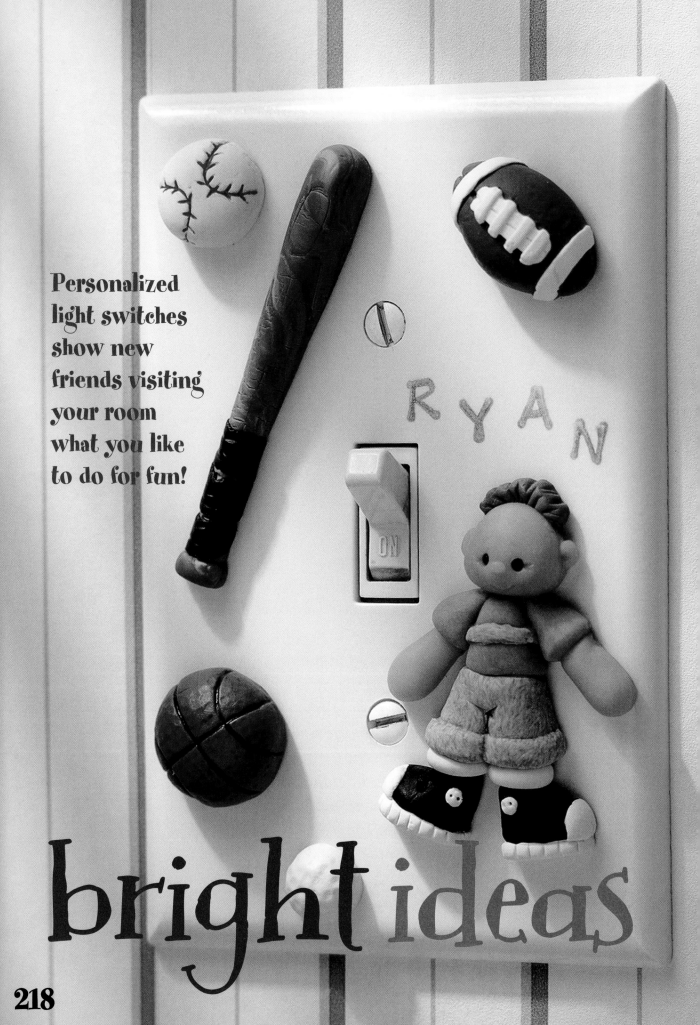

Personalized light switches show new friends visiting your room what you like to do for fun!

RYAN

ON

bright ideas

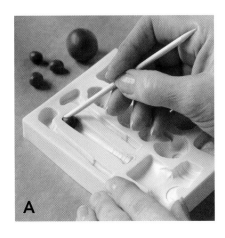

A

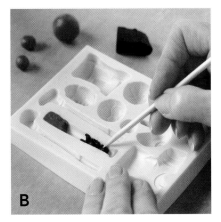

B

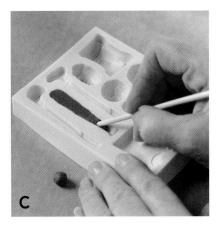

C

YOU'LL NEED

Waxed paper

Oven-bake clay, such as
Sculpey, (we used blue,
green, red, violet
Granitex, beige, black,
cadmium yellow, ecru,
orange, raw sienna,
and white)

Clay molds, such as
Sculpey Flexible Push
Molds (we used Family
Time, Grow a Garden,
and My Sports)

Clay shaper or
cuticle stick

Tiny black no-hole glass
beads for eyes

Needle tool

Purple telephone wire
for butterfly

White plastic light-switch
plate

Baking sheet covered
with parchment paper

Letter rubber stamps

Embossing ink in color
you like

Clear embossing powder

Heat gun

Acrylic paint in red
and black

Paper towels for the balls

Strong clear adhesive,
such as Super Glue gel

HERE'S HOW

1 Cover your work area
with waxed paper. Use
the color right out of the
package or mix clay
together to make the
colors you want. Knead
the clay in your hands until
it is soft and pliable. For
example, we mixed ecru
and cadmium yellow for
the girl's hair (*page 221*)

and raw sienna and
orange for the basketball,
opposite. To make the
bat look like wood,
roll together ecru and
raw sienna.

2 Refer to Photos A, B,
and C, *above*, to fill the
molds with the softened
clay. Begin with sections
that are at the bottom of
the mold, such as the
laces and stripes on the
football. Do not overfill
the sections because the
next layer of clay will push
up the layer below it
slightly. Use the end of a
clay shaper or cuticle stick
to push the clay into each
section and keep it away
from the next section.

continued on page 220

bright ideas

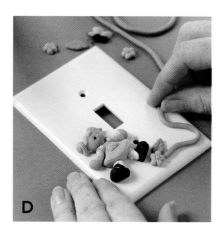

D

3 Fill the mold with the colors you like until the clay is level with the top edge of the mold.

4 Place the molds in the freezer for a few minutes. Pop out the clay pieces.

5 If you like, add details to your molded pieces, such as tiny black beads pushed into the face for eyes. Use additional clay to shape bangs and noses. Use the needle tool to draw the mouth, eye creases, eyelashes, and eyebrows, and to poke tiny holes in the buttons. For the butterfly antennae, curl ¾ inch lengths of wire and push them into the head.

6 Look at the photographs on *page 218* and *opposite*, and place the molded pieces on the switch plate. To make a vine, roll a long, thin green snake. Lay the vine on the switch plate (see Photo D). Lightly press all the pieces onto the plate.

7 Place the switch plate on a baking sheet covered with parchment paper. Ask a grown-up to put the baking sheet in the oven and bake the clay pieces according to the instructions on the clay package.

8 When the pieces are cool, stamp your name with embossing ink onto the switch plate. Carefully remove the baked clay pieces. Immediately sprinkle the wet inked name with clear embossing powder. Tap off the excess powder. Ask a grown-up to use the heat tool to melt the powder until it is shiny.

9 Put red paint in the baseball stitches and black paint the basketball seams. Dampen a paper towel with water and wipe off the extra paint. Let the paint dry.

10 Glue the baked clay pieces permanently onto the switch plate with strong adhesive.

OFF

MEGAN

crown jewelry holder

Wow! Shape a stunning jewelry holder that is fit for a queen.

jewelry

YOU'LL NEED

- 8×15- or 11×20-inch rectangle of tracing paper
- Pencil; scissors
- Gold screen
- Work gloves
- Utility scissors
- 24-gauge gold wire
- Glue gun and hot melt adhesive
- Sequined or pearl trim (1½ yards for the small crown and 2 yards for the large crown)
- 1¼-inch-wide gold-sequined elastic trim or 2-inch-wide pearl-edged ribbon (14 inches for the small crown or 22 inches for the large crown)

HERE'S HOW

1 Trace a large or small crown pattern, *page 225,* on one short side of the tracing paper. Connect the shapes on the dotted line and trace four more of the same pattern. Cut out the completed crown pattern.

continued on page 224

223

crown jewelry holder

2 Place the crown pattern on the gold screen. Ask a grown-up to wear gloves and use utility scissors to cut out the crown.

3 For a smooth bottom edge, put on gloves and fold up ½ to 1 inch along the long straight edge of the screen for the inside of the crown.

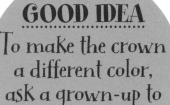

GOOD IDEA

To make the crown a different color, ask a grown-up to spray paint the screen.

4 Bend the screen into a circle so the bottom edges overlap a little. Weave gold wire through the two overlapped sides to keep the back edges together.

5 Curve the crown points outward. Ask a grown-up to hot-glue the sequined or pearl trim around the edges

of the points, beginning at the center back.

6 Ask a grown-up to help you hot-glue the sequined elastic trim or the wide-edge ribbon around the bottom of the crown. Overlap trim or ribbon ends at the center back.

224

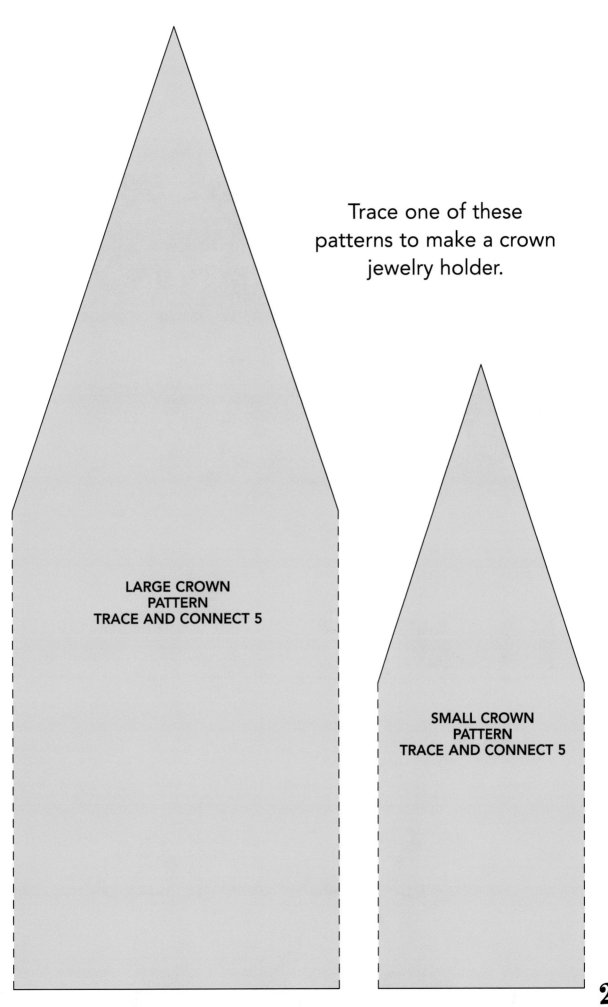

Trace one of these patterns to make a crown jewelry holder.

LARGE CROWN
PATTERN
TRACE AND CONNECT 5

SMALL CROWN
PATTERN
TRACE AND CONNECT 5

made for shades

It's always fun to show off a pretty glasses case, and these are sure to be show-offs. Made with bright foam pieces, beads, and laces, they will keep those shades from breaking.

YOU'LL NEED

For the star bead case
Crafts foam
Scissors; ruler
Ink pen or permanent
    marker
Small paper punch
30-inch piece of round
    flexible craft lacing
16 plastic 13-mm star
    beads

For the pony bead case
Crafts foam
30-inch piece of yellow
    round flexible lacing
32 plastic pony beads

HERE'S HOW

1 **For either project,**
use a ruler and pen to
measure and mark two
6¾×4-inch pieces on the
foam. Cut them out.

2 Start with one long
side of one piece of foam
and make a pen mark
every ½ inch, about ¼ inch
from the edge, as shown in
Photo A, *above right.* Do
the same on the other side
and at the bottom. Don't
mark the top of the foam.

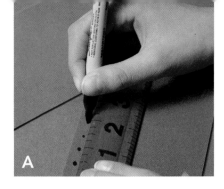

3 Use a paper punch to
punch holes where you
made ink marks.

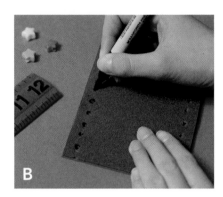

4 To mark the second
foam piece, lay the
punched piece over it with
the edges even. Put a pen
mark through each hole
(see Photo B). Punch the
holes with a paper punch.

5 Place one piece of
foam on top of the other
and match up the holes.
Push the lacing through
one set of top holes just

below the unpunched
edge. Knot the ends on
the back (see Photo C).
Push the long end of the
lacing back through the
first hole to the front.

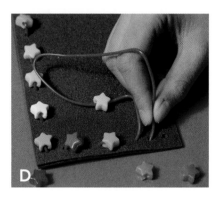

6 **For the star bead
case,** thread a star bead
on the lacing and push
the lacing through the
second hole. Bring the
lacing to the front through
the next hole and add
another star until all the
holes are laced.

For the pony bead case,
thread a pony bead on the
lacing. Bring the lacing
around the edge to the
back, come up through
the second hole, and add
another pony bead until
all the holes are laced.

7 When the last bead is
on, knot the lace on the
back side and clip the end
about ¼ inch from the knot.

Get a grip! These funky necklaces are made from pencil grippers and beads. You can string them on just about any kind of cord or ribbon.

easy-as-pie necklaces

HERE'S HOW

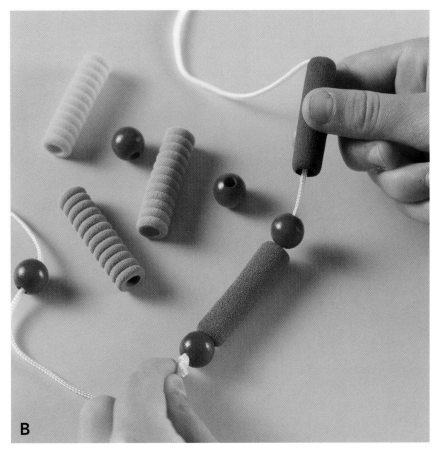

B

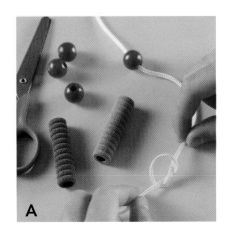

A

1 Decide how long you want the necklace. Cut a piece of cord 3 inches longer than that. Tie a double knot about ½ inch from the end.

2 Thread a bead. Tie another double knot next to the bead. Tie another double knot about 3 inches from the first bead. Start threading the beads and grippers, alternating beads and grippers until about 4 inches of cord remains as shown in Photo B.

3 Tie a double knot about ½ inch from the end to finish the end of the necklace.

GOOD IDEA
For a metallic necklace, go to the hardware store and buy small springs and lightweight washers.

229

bedazzling beads

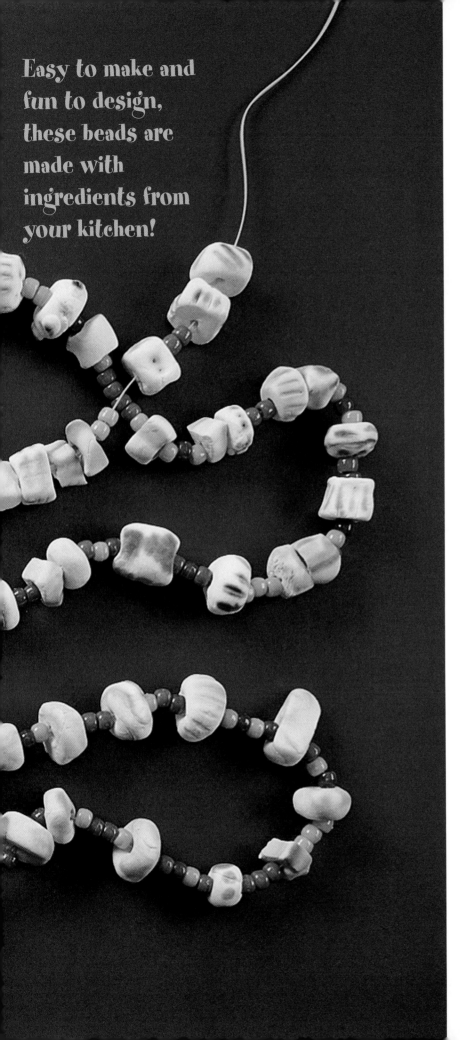

Easy to make and fun to design, these beads are made with ingredients from your kitchen!

YOU'LL NEED

A recipe of magic clay, *below*
Plastic drinking straws
Scissors; ruler
Food coloring
Flat pan or cookie sheet
Table knife; toothpicks
Yarn, plastic lacing, or string

Magic Clay
Sauce pan; damp cloth
2 cups baking soda
1 cup cornstarch
1¼ cups cold water
Aluminum foil

HERE'S HOW

1 Have a grown-up help you make the clay. You can keep the clay in a plastic

continued on page 232

GOOD IDEA
Be sure to cover your work surface before you begin because food coloring sometimes stains.

231

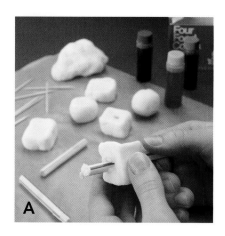

A

bag in the refrigerator if you want to make the beads later. (But don't let anyone eat it!)

Stir together the baking soda and cornstarch in a saucepan until it is all mixed up. Add the water and stir it again. Cook over medium heat, stirring constantly, until the mixture looks like moist mashed potatoes (about 10 or 15 minutes). Carefully pour it onto the foil and cover it with a damp cloth. Allow the clay to cool. When

B

cool, your clay is ready to make into beads. Keep the clay covered or in a plastic bag until you're ready to use it.

1 To make beads, break off a piece of the clay about the size of a large marble. Shape the bead however you wish.

2 Cut the plastic straws into pieces about 4 inches long. Use the straw to make the hole in the middle of the clay as shown in Photo A, *above left*.

The clay will get stuck in the middle of the straw. When that straw doesn't work any longer, use another piece of straw.

3 Use a toothpick dipped in food coloring to make lines and dots on the clay as shown in Photo B.

4 Lay the beads on a pan or cookie sheet to air dry. They will dry and be very hard in about 6 hours or overnight.

GOOD IDEA

If you cover your cookie sheet with foil, it will be easier to clean up!

C

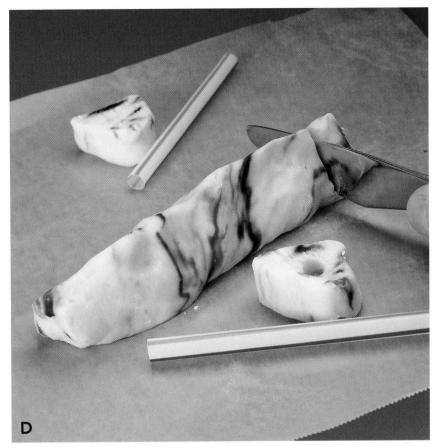

D

5 You can color the entire batch of clay any color or colors you want by adding food coloring and kneading it in. Or you can marbleize the clay like this: Shape a piece of clay into a hot dog bun shape. Put some food coloring in the middle and scrunch it all together as shown in Photo C. Shape it into a log shape for slicing, or just break off pieces of the clay to make beads.

6 If you slice the beads, slice them with a table knife as shown in Photo D. Slice the beads about ½ inch thick. Use the pieces of drinking straw to make the holes. Let these beads air-dry in a pan for about 6 hours or overnight.

7 After the beads are dry, thread them onto yarn, plastic lacing, or string. You can add colorful purchased beads between clay beads. Tie the ends of the yarn or string into a knot so the beads stay on.

GOOD IDEA
Because baking soda has a lot of salt in it, your hands will get dry. Keep some lotion handy.

charm cards

These charming necklaces do double duty as greeting cards. Depending on how you twist the pipe cleaners, you can make boy or girl charms.

Narrow pipe cleaners
Jump ring
Wood beads
¼-inch ribbon
Metal ball chain necklace
Card stock
Decorative paper
Scissors
Ruler
Glue stick
Tape

HERE'S HOW

1 Fold a pipe cleaner in half. Thread a jump ring on the center of the pipe cleaner. Thread both ends of the pipe cleaner through the wood bead for a head.

2 Bend out each pipe cleaner end at a 90-degree angle to make arms about ¾-inch long. Fold back the pipe cleaner arms to meet at the body. Twist the stem together once. Then form the remaining ends into a triangle skirt for the girl or inch-long legs that fold for the boy. For each one, twist the ends together and trim away leftover pipe cleaner. Make as many boy or girl charms as you want.

GOOD IDEA
String large alphabet beads between the charms to spell names or words.

3 Tie a small bow around the waists of the girl charms. Thread the girl or boy charms onto the metal ball chain.

4 To make a card, fold a 5×8-inch piece of card stock in half. Glue one or two rectangles of decorative paper on the front of the card. Make two small slits in the top of the card. Thread each end of the chain through the slits. Clasp the chain behind the card and wind up the extra ball chain and loosely tape it behind the front of the card.

nifty necklace

Use this fun technique to make a
necklace to match any outfit.

YOU'LL NEED

Air-dry clay, such as
   Crayola Model Magic
Plastic straws in several
   colors
Washable paints
Paintbrush
Scissors
Colored paper clips
Plastic lanyard long
   enough to fit
   around neck

HERE'S HOW

1 Pinch small pieces of the clay as shown on the necklace, *opposite*. Poke a hole in each piece with a straw. Paint them and make patterns on the pieces with a straw or pencil. Let the clay dry.

2 Cut some of the plastic straws into short pieces.

3 When the clay is dry, line up the painted pieces, the straw pieces, and paper clips the way you want them on the necklace.

4 String the pieces onto two pieces of lanyard. Tie a knot at each end. Tie the ends together to form a necklace.

GOOD IDEA

Choose wood or plastic beads bigger than the straws to use on your necklace.

funky barrettes

You'll be totally cool when you wear these barrettes made from the most unexpected things you find around the house!

YOU'LL NEED

For sunglasses barrette
Inexpensive sunglasses
Tiny screwdriver,
   if needed
Sandpaper
Thick white crafts glue
Assorted beads
Buttons in fun shapes
Barrette back
For comb barrette
Small comb
Sandpaper
Embroidery floss
   and needle

Assorted beads
Thick white crafts
   glue
Flower-shape button
Barrette back

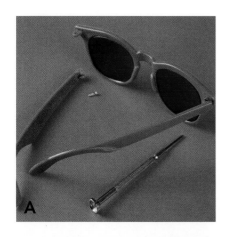

A

B

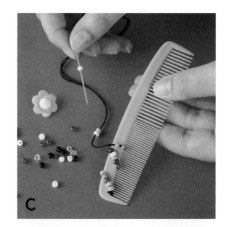

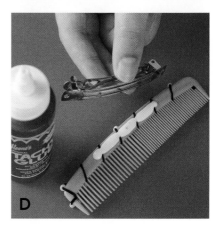

C

D

3 Glue beads and buttons across the top of the glasses. Let the glue dry. Glue the barrette back to the back of the sunglasses.

For comb barrette

1 Sand the back of the comb slightly.

2 Thread the needle with three strands of embroidery floss. Tie the end tightly to one end of the comb. String beads on the floss and wind it around the comb (see Photo C). Clip the floss, leaving enough to tie at the other end. Tie the floss tightly.

3 Put small dabs of glue under the beads. Glue the button to the teeth of the comb.

4 Glue the barrette back to the back of the comb (see Photo D).

HERE'S HOW

For sunglasses barrette

1 Ask a grown-up to remove the sides of the sunglasses, as shown in Photo A, with a tiny screwdriver, or pop them off.

2 Sand the back of the sunglasses a little to roughen the plastic (see Photo B) to make the barrette back stick.

239

try something new

You've learned all the basics, you're a crafting pro—now onto these projects that add to the glow! Make a pretty barrette or a blooming place mat. Emboss a card or make a star-dotted hat! From a lamp to a scrapbook, whatever you choose, with all these great projects you just can't loose!

(it'll be FUN!)

TO MOM

glamour ring

Every finger deserves such a button beauty! So easy to make you'll want to give some to your friends!

B

A

YOU'LL NEED

Utility scissors
Pipe cleaners
Decorative shank buttons

HERE'S HOW

1 For each ring, cut a piece of pipe cleaner 4 inches long. Thread a button onto the pipe cleaner and push the button to the center as shown in Photo A, *above*.

2 Wrap the pipe cleaner around your finger to shape the ring. Twist the ends of the pipe cleaner once to make it the right size as shown in Photo B.

GOOD IDEA
Be sure to tuck in the ends of the pipe cleaner wire so they don't poke you.

3 Take the ring off your finger and trim the ends of the pipe cleaner about ¼ inch long. Twist the trimmed pipe cleaner ends around the rest of the pipe cleaner ring to hold the ends in place.

mama & baby

Our mama is so proud of her baby, she carries her little one with her everywhere she goes. You can make this soft, cuddly couple using felt, floss, and yarn.

YOU'LL NEED

Pencil; tracing paper

Scissors

Two 9×12-inch pieces of purple felt

Two 9×12-inch pieces of pink felt

9×12-inch piece of black felt

9×12-inch piece of skin color felt

Scrap of white felt

Fabric glue

Black thread

Cotton embroidery floss in red and purple

Straight pins; tapestry needle; fiberfill stuffing

Two 6-inch-long strands of rug yarn for hair

4 inches of ⅛-inch-wide pink ribbon

6 assorted buttons

Cotton swab

Powder blush

NOTE

There is only one sleeve piece because the mama's left arm becomes the baby.

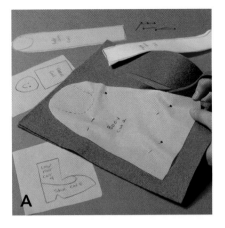

A

HERE'S HOW

1 Trace patterns, *pages 248–249*, onto tracing paper; cut out. Cut bodies and sleeve from purple felt; leg/foot pieces, right arms, and faces from pink felt; shoes from black felt; and left arms from skin color felt as shown in Photo A, *above*.

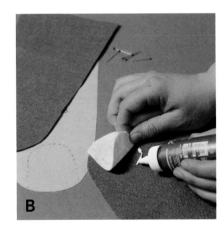

B

2 Glue the mama's face to one of the purple body pieces as shown in Photo B. Cut two pea-size circles from black felt and glue them to the face for eyes. Cut two tiny snips of white felt and glue to the eyes as shown in the photo, *opposite*. Cut a 1½-inch piece of black thread, dip it in glue, and shape it into a curve on the face to make the nose (see Mama's Face pattern on *page 248*). Make the mouth in the same way using 1½ inches of red floss.

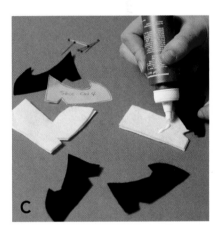

C

3 Glue two leg/foot pieces back to back to make each leg as shown in Photo C. Glue a shoe to both sides of each leg/foot piece.

continued on page 246

245

mama & baby

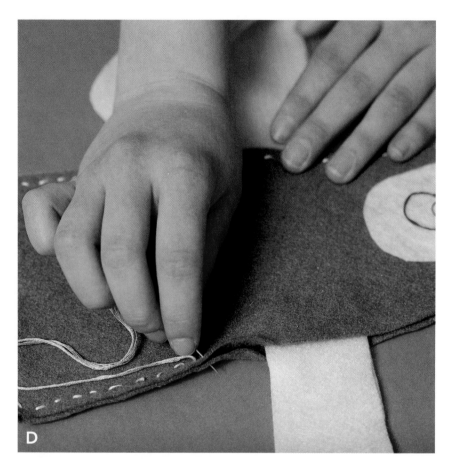

7 Stuff the body with fiberfill (see Photo E). Sew the opening closed.

8 Untwist the rug yarn pieces. Tie a knot in both ends of each piece. Glue the pieces across the top

4 Glue the right arm pieces and the left arm pieces back to back.

5 Pin the body front to back. Insert the arms and legs between the dots on the pattern. Make sure the thumb on the right arm points up.

6 Thread the needle with a strand of purple floss. Sew the body together with a running stitch (see Step 1 and Step 2, *right*) around the edge as shown in Photo D. Leave an opening across the top of the head for stuffing.

RUNNING STITCH

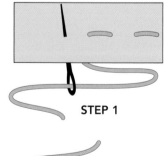

STEP 1

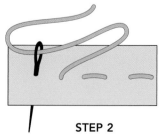

STEP 2

of the head for hair. Use as many pieces as you wish.

9 Glue the baby's face to the front side of the left arm. Cut two tiny black felt circles and glue them to the face for eyes. Dip a ¾-inch piece of red floss in glue and place it on the face for a mouth. Clip a 1½-inch piece of yarn. Tie a bow in the center of the yarn with pink ribbon and glue it to the top of the baby's head.

10 Glue the sleeve to the upper back of the right arm.

11 Cross the left arm over the right arm. Fold the end of the left arm up and underneath the right arm so the baby's face peeks out over the right arm (see Photo F). Flip up the right hand over the bottom of the baby (left arm) and glue it in place.

F

12 Glue the buttons to the front of mama's dress to make polka dots.

13 Rub the cotton swab in powder blush and use it to make rosy cheeks on both of the faces (see the photo on *page 244*).

continued on page 248

mama & baby

**MAMA'S FACE
CUT 1**

**BABY'S FACE
CUT 1**

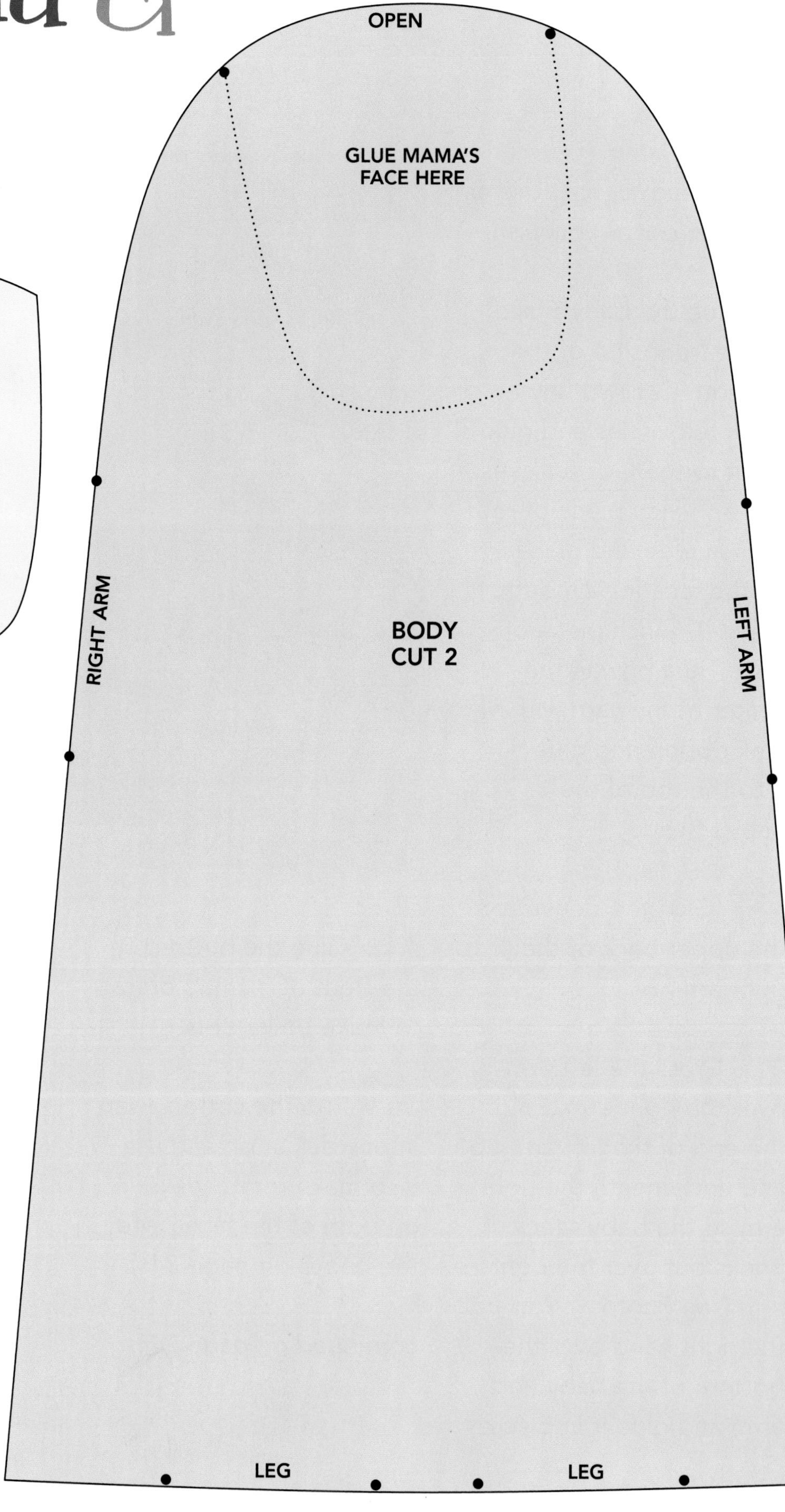

OPEN

GLUE MAMA'S
FACE HERE

RIGHT ARM

LEFT ARM

BODY
CUT 2

LEG

LEG

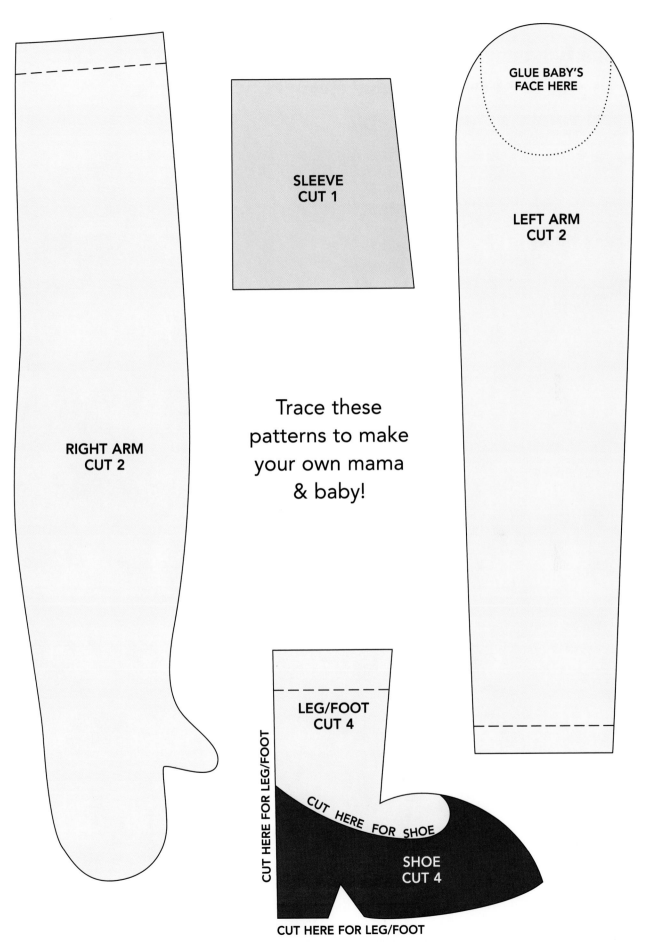

RIGHT ARM
CUT 2

SLEEVE
CUT 1

GLUE BABY'S
FACE HERE

LEFT ARM
CUT 2

Trace these
patterns to make
your own mama
& baby!

LEG/FOOT
CUT 4

CUT HERE FOR LEG/FOOT

CUT HERE FOR SHOE

SHOE
CUT 4

CUT HERE FOR LEG/FOOT

249

Simply creepy, these finger puppets are a cinch to make! All you need are some pipe cleaners, wiggle eyes, and your very own fingers.

creepy
crawlers

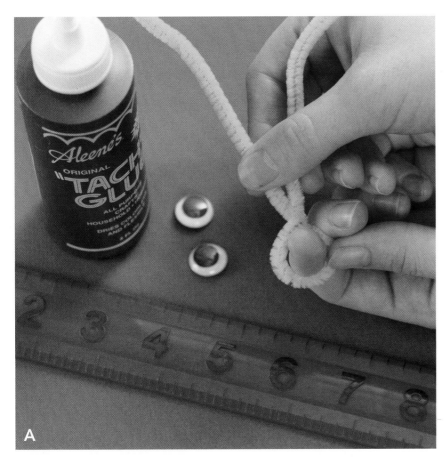

A

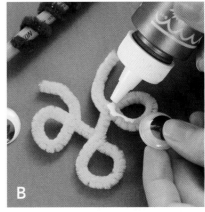

B

YOU'LL NEED

**Pipe cleaners in
 assorted colors**
Wiggle eyes
Thick white crafts glue

HERE'S HOW

1 Make a loop in the pipe cleaner for your finger in the middle of the pipe cleaner as shown in Photo A, *above*. Wrap the pipe cleaner around your finger and twist it to stay in place. To make eyes, loop the pipe cleaner around your finger about 1 inch from the first loop and twist in place. Make another loop for the other eye.

2 Glue the wiggly eyes to the eye holes as shown in Photo B.

3 Bend and twist the pipe cleaners to make each creepy crawler different. Try these ideas: To make corkscrew hair, wrap a pipe cleaner around a pencil. To make big ears, make long loops and glue the ends behind each eye.

GOOD IDEA
Glue on small pom-poms, sequins, or jewels to dress up your crawlers.

my special scrapbook

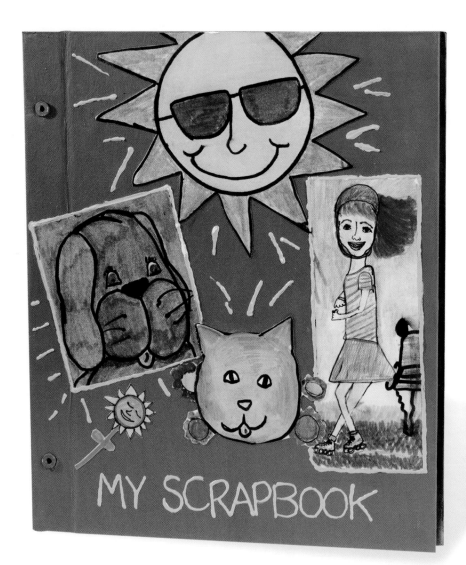

Use your own favorite drawings to make a cool cover for a scrapbook or diary.

YOU'LL NEED

Newspapers
Scissors
Your own drawings or
    artwork
Scrapbook
Purple acrylic paint or
    any color you like
Foam plate
Paintbrush
Decoupage medium,
    such as Mod Podge
Pencil
Tube-style paint in yellow
    or any color you like

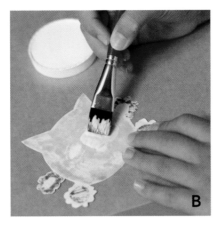

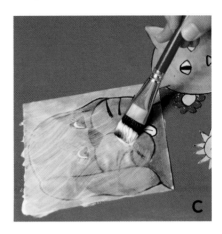

HERE'S HOW

1 Cover your work surface with newspapers. Cut out your drawings. Put them on the scrapbook and arrange them however you like. Take off the drawings.

2 Put some acrylic paint on a foam plate. Paint the entire cover of your scrapbook as shown in Photo A, *above*. Let the paint dry. (If it looks streaky, you can apply another coat of paint.) Clean your brush very well in water. Let the paint dry.

3 Pour some decoupage medium into the lid. Use a paintbrush to coat the back of your drawing with decoupage medium as shown in Photo B. Cover the whole piece of paper well. Before the decoupage medium dries, turn the artwork over and put it on your book cover. To smooth out wrinkles, press them down firmly with the paintbrush. Decoupage all of your drawings this way.

4 When the drawings feel dry to the touch, coat the entire scrapbook cover with decoupage medium as shown in Photo C. (The decoupage looks white when it's wet, but it will dry clear.) (Write your letters in pencil first.

If you make a mistake with a pencil, it will wipe off with a wet napkin.) Use a bottle of yellow fabric paint to write "MY SCRAPBOOK." Outline your pictures or make lines, dots, or squiggles.

GOOD IDEA
Don't use drawings made with washable markers because they may smear.

year-round greeting cards

Let someone know how special you think they are with a cheerful greeting card that's made by you—especially for them!

YOU'LL NEED

Colored card paper
Envelopes to fit cards
Tracing paper
Pencil
Scissors: straight, decorative-edge, and pinking shears
Wrapping paper or decorative papers for memory books
Glue stick
Marking and paint pens
Fabric paint
Paper doilies

HERE'S HOW

Fold the paper for the card in half and cut it in a square or rectangle to fit inside the envelope.

1 **For the birthday card,** trace the patterns, *page 256,* onto tracing paper and cut them out.

2 Trace around the candle patterns on the decorative paper as many times as you wish. Glue the candles on the front of the card.

3 For each candle flame trace around the pattern on yellow paper. Cut out the flame shapes and glue them on the candles. Write a message with a paint pen.

4 **For the Easter card,** cut a rectangle slightly smaller than the folded card with decorative-edge or straight scissors.

5 Trace and cut out the patterns on *page 257.* Trace around the patterns on papers and cut out. Cut fringes in the grass.

6 Glue the pieces in place as shown, *opposite.* Glue the beak to the head, and the head to the body. Do not glue the chick to the card. Glue only the bottom edge of the egg so the chick can slip in and out.

7 **For the Christmas card,** cut rectangles from white paper. With a paint pen, write "Merry Christmas" on the paper in various languages (Feliz

Navidad is Spanish, Mele Kalikimaka is Hawaiian, and Joyeux Noel is French).

8 Let the paint dry. Glue the messages on the card. Outline the rectangles with a paint pen.

9 **For the Valentine's Day card,** write "I Love You" with bright red fabric paint on a white doily. Let the paint dry.

10 Glue the doily on the front of the card and let the glue dry.

continued on page 256

year-round greeting cards

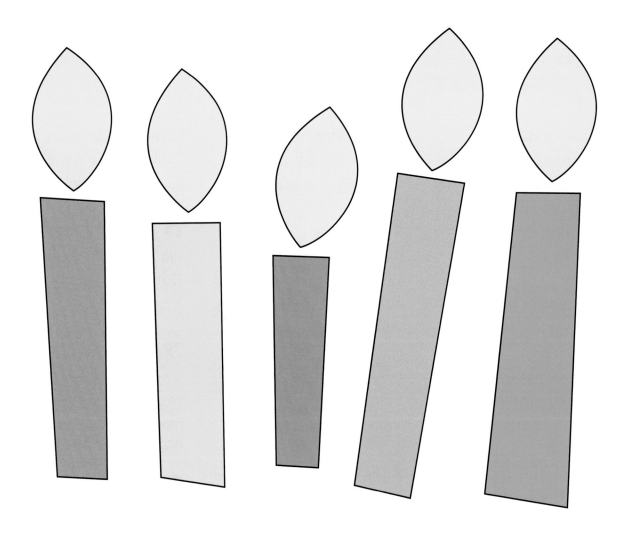

HAPPY BIRTHDAY CARD PATTERNS

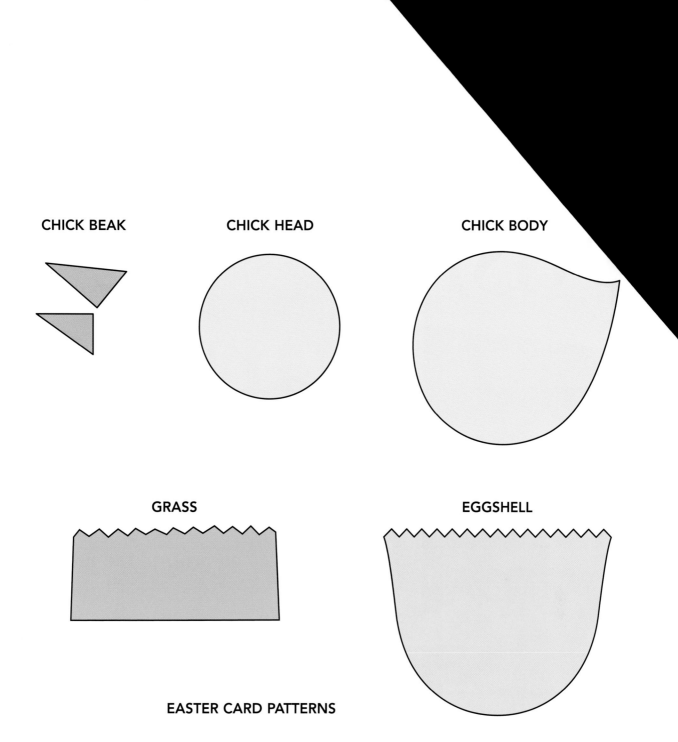

CHICK BEAK

CHICK HEAD

CHICK BODY

GRASS

EGGSHELL

EASTER CARD PATTERNS

petal
er
candles

Add pretty blooms to
plain candles by
pressing tacks and pins
all around the pillars.

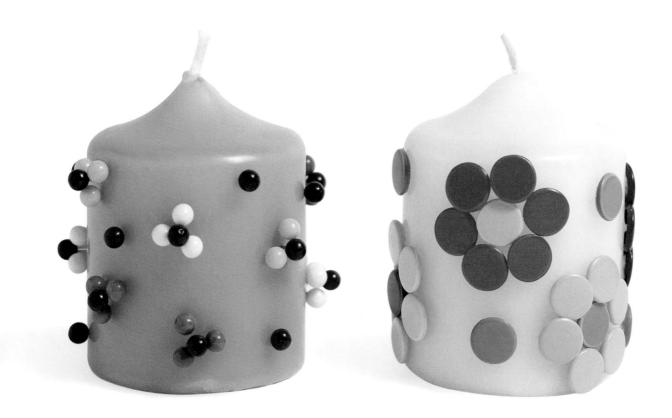

YOU'LL NEED

Pillar candle
Push-pins, map pins, or
thumbtacks

HERE'S HOW

1 Push a pin or tack into the candle as shown in Photo A, *right*, for the flower center. Choose another color pin or tack to make petals. Push each into the candle around the flower center pin (see Photo B).

A

B

2 Space flowers as far apart as you wish. To add stems, use green map pins. You can make flowers all around the candle or only on one side.

3 Put the candle in a candleholder. Ask a grown-up to light your candle for everyone to enjoy. Never leave candles burning when no one is in the room.

259

my special chair

You'll be sittin' pretty in this adorable armchair that shows off your creativity and artistic talents.

YOU'LL NEED

**A chair just your size that
can be upholstered**
**White canvas, enough to
upholster a chair**
Drop cloth
**Paint pens and
permanent
markers**

HERE'S HOW

1 Ask a grown-up to
figure out how much
canvas is needed to cover
the chair. Lay the fabric on
a drop-cloth-covered floor.

2 Draw pictures and
write messages on the
fabric with paint pens and
permanent markers. (Have
friends or family members
help you if you want.) Let
the paint and markers dry.

3 Ask a grown-up to
take the fabric and the
chair to an upholstery
shop. The upholsterer
will cover the chair with
the unique fabric you
have created.

GOOD IDEA
For a quicker
project, buy a small
pillow and draw on
it with marking
pens.

Rubber stamp kids on paper and make your own scrapbook and bookmark.

FRIENDS FOREVER

Kids rubber stamping

YOU'LL NEED

Fiskars small paper cutter
8½×11-inch sheets of
    gray, white, and cream
    card stock (or the
    colors you want)
Small rubber stamps,
    such as flowers, hearts,
    stars, and a sun
White opaque ink pad
Rubber stamps of kids or
    other designs
Black dye ink pad
Colored pencils, marker,
    or crayons
Scissors
½ inch dimensional
    self-stick dots
Small sticker letters
⅛-inch hole punch
1 yard of narrow cording

A

HERE'S HOW

1 Ask a grown-up to use
the small paper cutter to
cut one sheet of gray card
stock in half for the cover.
The piece should measure
5½×8½ inches. Press
the small stamp or stamps
on the opaque white ink
pad. One at a time, press
the stamps on one side of
the paper. If you wish,
stamp all over the paper
to make a pale design or
re-ink the stamp after
each print.

2 For the cover design,
generously ink one of the
stamps of your choice with
black. Firmly press the
stamp on a sheet of white
card stock and be careful
not to move the stamp

continued on page 264

Kids rubber stamping

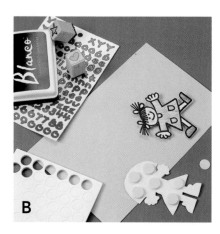

B

once you press it on the paper. Carefully lift up the stamp to keep from smearing the ink. Stamp one or more stamps on the same piece of paper.

3 Use colored pencils, crayons, or markers to color in the figures however you want. Add dots and stripes to the clothing as you like. Use scissors to cut around the figures.

C

4 Remove the protective paper from one side of several dimensional dots. Press the dots on the back of the paper kids as shown in Photo B. Remove the other piece of protective paper, position the kids on the cover, and press. Press sticker letters on the cover.

5 To make each page for the scrapbook, ask a grown-up to cut white card stock in half with the small paper cutter. Decorate the pages however you want, or just leave the pages blank to decorate later. See the page in Photo C for an idea how to decorate the pages.

D

E

7 Place the binding over the book. Insert the narrow cording through the holes from back to front as shown in Photo E. Tie the cording into a bow on the front of the book.

6 Cut a 2×5½-inch strip from cream card stock. Fold the strip in half to make a 1×5½-inch binding. Measure 1½ inch in from each end of the binding and ½ inch from the fold. Use the ⅛-inch hole punch to punch through both layers of the binding as shown in Photo D. Stack the front cover, the pages, and the back cover together. Use the hole punch to make holes through the covers and pages in the same places as for the binding.

GOOD IDEA
Use rubber stamps to decorate gift tags, greeting cards, postcards, and paper bags.

265

fairest-of-all mirror set

Pretend you're a princess or queen when you look into this magical mirror trimmed with swirling colors of yarn.

YOU'LL NEED

Thick white crafts glue
Handheld mirror, brush, and
    comb set with smooth, flat
    surfaces
Paintbrush; scissors
Yarns in your favorite
    colors; jewels

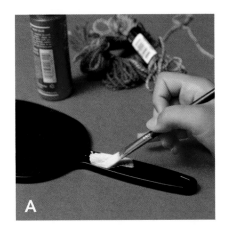
A

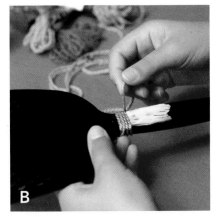
B

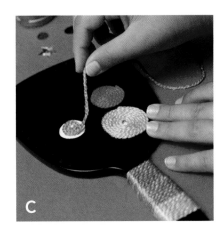
C

HERE'S HOW

1 Dab glue on the top of the mirror handle and smear it around with a paintbrush or your finger as shown in Photo A, *above*.

2 Begin at the top of the handle, place the yarn on the glue, and wind the yarn around to cover the entire handle (see Photo B). Add glue as you wind. You can use one color of yarn or several different colors.

3 Cover the back of the mirror with a thin layer of glue; wind the yarn on the glued area (see Photo C).

4 You can wind yarn in any shapes you like.

Keep adding colors around the shapes until the whole area is covered. Glue on some jewels.

5 Decorate the hairbrush and the comb using yarn and jewels.

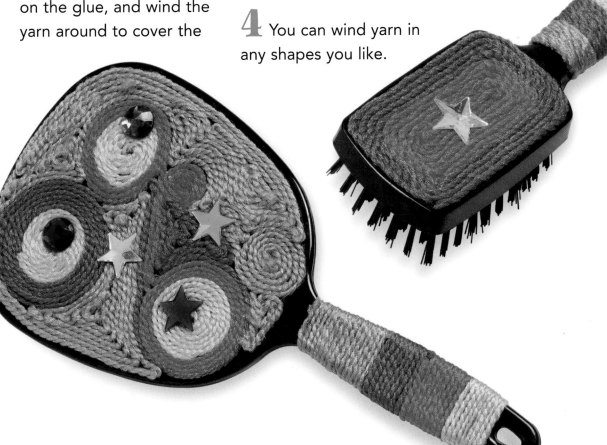

nature caps

Before you go out to play, pull on a fun hat covered with bright felt shapes!

BUTTER
AND MO
A Study of the Largest and Most Bea

A

GOOD IDEA

Use permanent marker or paint pen to make eyes or other details on the shapes.

YOU'LL NEED

Tracing paper
Pencil
Index cards
Scissors
Scraps of felt in various
   colors
Hole punch (for star cap)
Cotton baseball cap
Hand towel
Narrow rickrack
Extra-tacky crafts glue

HERE'S HOW

1 Use a pencil to trace the star, butterfly, or any of the patterns from *pages 270–273* onto tracing paper. Trace each of the pieces separately if the shape has more than one part. Place each traced pattern on an index card and draw around it again. Cut it out. This will make a heavier pattern to trace around on your felt.

2 Place the pattern shapes on the felt pieces. Draw around them, as shown in Photo A, *above.* Use the hole punch to make felt dots for the stars if you wish.

continued on page 270

nature caps

5 Glue felt dots on each star (see Photo B). For other layered designs, glue the felt pieces on top of one another as shown on the pattern, *below.*

6 Glue the felt pieces to the cap, using the photograph on *page 268* as a guide to help you decide where to put the shapes.

3 Stuff the cap firmly with the towel so the crown holds its shape, making it easier to glue on the rickrack or the felt shapes.

4 To add rickrack, glue it along the seams on the crown and around the bill where it joins the crown.

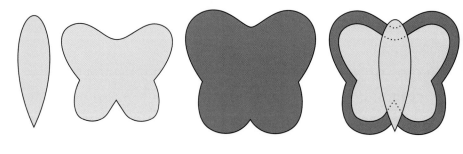

BUTTERFLY

Here is an example of how to cut out and glue layered pattern pieces!

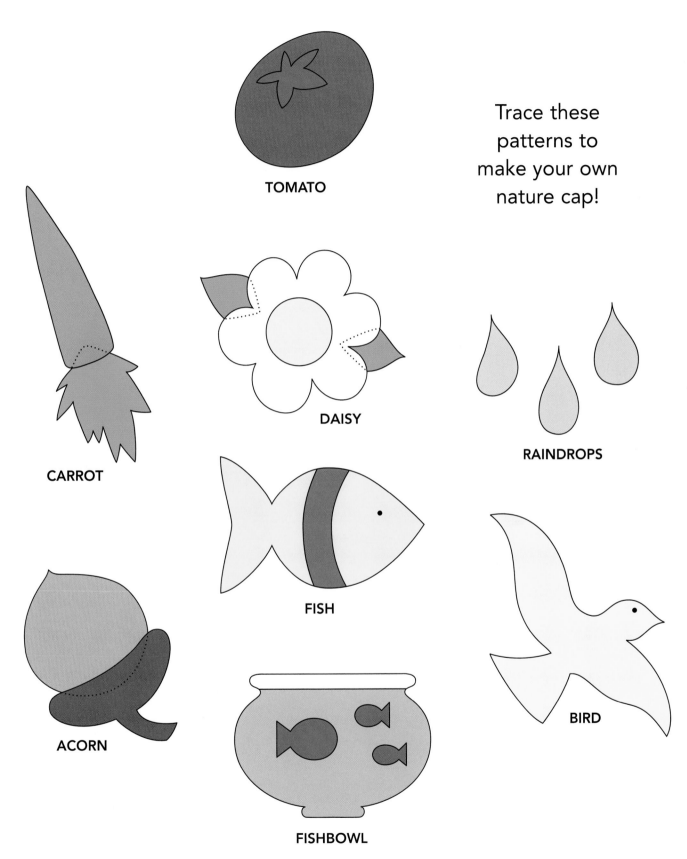

TOMATO

Trace these patterns to make your own nature cap!

CARROT

DAISY

RAINDROPS

ACORN

FISH

FISHBOWL

BIRD

continued on page 272

nature caps

Trace these patterns to make your own nature cap!

SPIDER

APPLE

SUN

TREE

WORM

SUNGLASSES

UMBRELLA

TULIP

LEAF

TURTLE

PALM TREE

EVERGREEN

HEART

STAR

MUSHROOM

BUTTERFLY

273

cross-stitch trinket box

A great beginner's project, this cheerful cross-stitched nature box can hide the tiniest treasures.

YOU'LL NEED

7-count plastic canvas
Ruler
Scissors
Cotton embroidery floss
   in colors listed in the
   key on *page 277*
Needle
Tape
Felt
Iron-on adhesive, such as
   Heat 'n' Bond
Iron

HERE'S HOW

1 Cut six 22×22-hole pieces of plastic canvas (this measures about 3⅜×3⅜ inches square). Trim away rough edges so the thread does not catch on them as you stitch.

2 Thread a needle with a double strand of floss. Draw the thread ends together and tape them down on the back side of the canvas near the beginning of the stitch area. Taping will control the thread for beginners better than trying to hold down the thread while you stitch.

3 Find the center of one chart and the center of one square of canvas. Work half cross-stitches in one direction, then finish the cross-stitch by working back over the half cross-stitches. Be sure to work over the taped end of the thread to tack it in place.

4 When an area is done or the thread becomes short, run the needle under a few stitches on the back side of the canvas to tack it down. Cut the thread end. Rethread the needle to finish the designs.

continued on page 276

275

cross-stitch trinket box

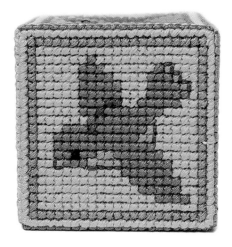

5 For the border, use the background floss color to whipstitch across the outside edge in one direction, then work back across in the opposite direction. Work two whipstitches in each corner hole. Tack the thread ends.

6 To finish cut six 3¼×3¼-inch pieces of felt and six 3¼×3¼-inch pieces of Heat 'n' Bond. Bond the backing to the felt as directed. To bond felt to the cross-stitch piece, place it on the wrong side of the canvas. Ask a grown-up to use the steam setting on an iron to go through the felt and hold it for 10 seconds.

7 To assemble the box, lay out the squares. Place two squares with right sides together. Use two

strands of floss to whipstitch the sides together. Repeat until all four side pieces are joined in a row. Form a square by bringing the ends together with right sides facing out. Sew the sides together with blind stitches. Blindstitch the base to the bottom of the squares. Whipstitch the lid on the outside of the design.

Anchor		DMC
002	•	000 White
403	■	310 Black
371	#	433 Chestnut
046	×	666 True red
256	I	704 Chartreuse
304	+	741 Tangerine
054	▽	956 Geranium
297	−	973 True canary
100	▲	3837 Lavender
1089	○	3845 Turquoise

BACKSTITCH

403 / 310 Black –
antennae on butterfly

403 / 433 Chestnut – bird

CROSS-STITCH DIAGRAMS   WHIPSTITCH
DIAGRAM

BLIND STITCH
DIAGRAM

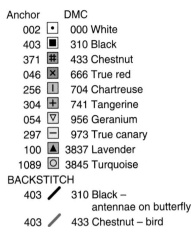
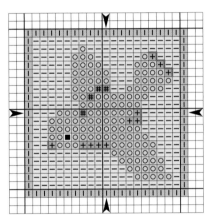
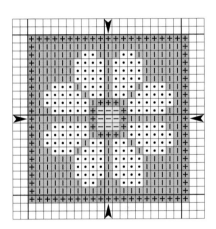

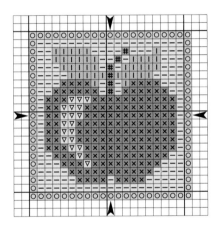
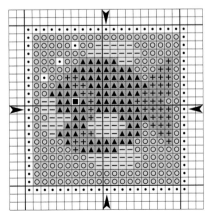
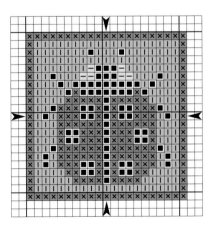

perk-me-up barrettes

When you want to pull back your hair during sunny weather, these pretty hair trims are the perfect finishing touch for springtime dress.

frilly flower barrette

YOU'LL NEED

1-inch peach button
⅝-inch yellow button
⅜-inch pink button
Thin pipe cleaners
  in purple, orange,
  and yellow
Regular pipe cleaners
  in pink and green
Ice pick
Hot-glue gun and
  hot-glue sticks
Barrette back

HERE'S HOW

1 Stack the buttons with the largest on the bottom. From the bottom, push a purple pipe cleaner through a hole in each button. Slide buttons to the center of the pipe cleaner. Poke the end of the pipe cleaner back through the other hole. If the buttons have four holes, repeat the process.

2 Fold the pink, orange, green, and yellow pipe cleaners in half. Tightly twist the purple pipe cleaner around the other pipe cleaner centers.

3 Shape the ends of the green pipe cleaner into leaves. Ask a grown-up to wrap the remaining pipe cleaners around an ice pick to curl.

4 Hot-glue the decoration to a barrette back. Let the glue set.

bow barrette

YOU'LL NEED

1½-inch ribbon
Barrette back
Scissors
Flat marble
Hot-glue gun and
   hot-glue sticks

GOOD IDEA
Glue buttons, clip earrings, appliqués, or silk flowers to the center of the barrette bow.

HERE'S HOW

1 Wrap ribbon around the barrette top to cover it. Glue the ribbon ends on the back side. Slip another piece of ribbon under the center wraps. Tie it into a bow.

2 Glue a marble in the center of the bow. Trim the ribbon ends.

continued on page 280

279

perk-me-up barrettes

ribbon barrette

YOU'LL NEED

⅛-inch satin ribbons
Ruler
Scissors
Barrette back

HERE'S HOW

1 Cut ribbons into 5-inch lengths. Tie them around the barrette top and knot them. Trim the ribbon ends if you want.

GOOD IDEA
To make two gifts in one, use these festive barrettes for package toppers.

butterfly barrette

YOU'LL NEED

Barrette back
Artificial butterfly
Silicone glue

HERE'S HOW

1 Decide where to place the butterfly on the barrette.

2 Put a line of glue along the barrette and be careful not to get any glue on the hinge. Gently press the butterfly in place. Let the glue dry.

jeweled barrette

YOU'LL NEED

Pliers
Clip earrings
Emery board
Hot-glue gun and
   hot-glue sticks
Barrette back

HERE'S HOW

1 Use pliers to remove the clips from the earrings. Sand any rough edges with an emery board.

2 Arrange and glue the earrings on the barrette top. Let the glue dry.

GOOD IDEA
String beads on wire, coil them into small circles, twist the ends, and glue it on the barrette.

pasta frames

Wonderful for framing your works of art, these fun frames can be whipped up with a few supplies found at home.

YOU'LL NEED

**Frame with wide
  flat surface**
Newspapers
Thick white crafts glue
Pasta rings or couscous
**Cream-color
  acrylic paint**
Paintbrush
**Shoe polish in blue
  or brown**
Rag
Clear varnish or sealer

HERE'S HOW

1 Ask a grown-up to remove the glass and backing from the frame. Lay frame flat on a paper-covered work surface. Spread an even, thick layer of glue on the surface of the frame.

Sprinkle or arrange the pasta on the wet glue as shown in Photo A, *right.* Let the glue dry.

2 Paint the entire frame with cream-color acrylic paint. Let the paint dry. Paint another coat if needed. Let the paint dry.

3 Coat the entire frame with shoe polish in blue or brown as shown in Photo B. Dab off extra shoe polish with a rag, wiping enough off to leave the raised area a light color and the crevices a darker color. Let the polish dry.

4 Paint a coat of clear varnish or sealer over the entire frame. Let it dry.

A

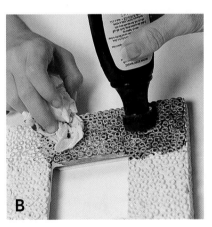

B

283

springtime
napkin
rings

It takes little time to braid up a table full of these pretty napkin rings.

YOU'LL NEED

3 colors of pipe cleaners
Ruler
Paper towel tube

HERE'S HOW

1 Choose six pipe cleaners, two of each color. With like colors together, even up the ends of pipe cleaners. Leave 3 inches at one end and begin to braid the pipe cleaners. Stop braiding 3 inches from the opposite end.

2 For looped ends, bend over the pipe cleaners to form loops. Wrap a separate pipe cleaner around the ends. Tuck the end of the pipe cleaner into the wraps.

3 For wrapped ends, braid the entire length of six pipe cleaners. Wrap the ends tightly with a separate pipe cleaner.

4 To shape the pipe cleaners in a circle, wrap braided pipe cleaners around a paper tube.

GOOD IDEA
Make napkin rings for each holiday by using different colors of pipe cleaners.

blooming place mats

Make every meal a special event with these colorful mats placed on the table.

BLOOMING
PLACE
MATS WHITE
FLOWER
PATTERN

HERE'S HOW

1 Trace the patterns, *left* and *pages 288–289*. Cut out. Trace around the pattern pieces on foam. Cut out the shapes.

2 Bend pipe cleaners into stems. Glue them on the foam place mat, bending the ends to the mat back. If making the yellow flower, bend purple pipe cleaners as shown in the photo, *opposite*.

3 Look at the photo, *opposite*, and glue the foam pieces in place to make flowers. Glue on leaves. Let the glue dry.

continued on page 288

YOU'LL NEED

Pencil and tracing paper
Scissors
Crafting foam in white, yellow, green, and red-pink

Pipe cleaners in green and purple
Silicone glue
Foam place mats in any color

287

blooming place mats

**BLOOMING
PLACE MATS
RED-PINK
FLOWER
PATTERN**

BLOOMING
PLACE MATS
YELLOW
FLOWER
PATTERN

GOOD IDEA
Use a roll of woven
foam drawer liner
to make a table
runner similar to
the place mats.

289

Whether used to add decorative stripes to a shaker or for making the pleasant twangs of a string instrument, rubber bands are a hit in this musical duo.

rubber band band

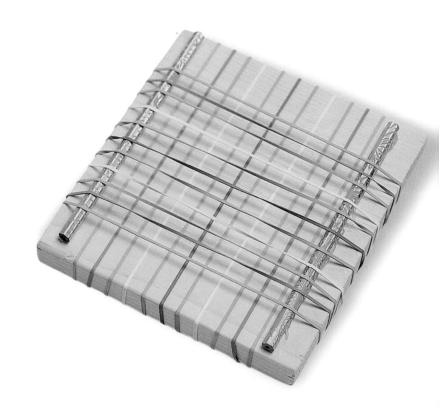

stringed instrument

YOU'LL NEED

2 decorative pencils
Hacksaw
7×7-inch piece of wood
Hot-glue gun and
  hot-glue sticks
Colored rubber bands

HERE'S HOW

1 Ask a grown-up to saw the eraser ends off two pencils. Also have a grown-up hot-glue the pencils to two sides of the wood piece as shown in the photo, *opposite*. Let the glue dry.

2 Place rubber bands over the wood, parallel to the pencils. Place rubber bands over the wood piece in the opposite direction, so they rest on the pencils. To make sounds, pluck or strum the top layer of rubber bands.

shaker

YOU'LL NEED

1 cup uncooked popcorn,
  rice, or dried beans
Tall stacked-chip
  container with lid
Packing tape
Ice pick
Pencil
Jute rope
Scissors
Hot-glue gun and
  hot-glue sticks
Colored rubber bands
Fine, metallic colored
  wire
Wire cutters
Ruler

HERE'S HOW

1 Place popcorn, rice, or dried beans in the container. Tape the lid to the container. Ask a grown-up to use an ice pick to poke a hole in the center of the lid. Make the hole larger with a pencil.

2 Place the end of the jute into the hole in the lid. Begin wrapping the jute around and around, gluing as you wrap. Wrap the lid, sides, and bottom of the container until it is all covered. Clip the jute and glue the end to hold it in place.

3 To make rubber band bows, hold a dozen rubber bands. Wrap the center with a 6-inch length of wire to hold them tight. Make three bows. Glue the bows on the shaker.

leather lace flowerpot

Give a fresh look to a terra-cotta flowerpot by adding stripes and swirls of colorful leather.

YOU'LL NEED

Terra-cotta flowerpot
Ruler
Leather lace in colors
  you like
Scissors
Thick white crafts glue

HERE'S HOW

1 Measure the rim of the flowerpot. Use this measurement to cut about 100 pieces from leather lace.

2 Glue the lace pieces vertically (up and down) around the rim of the flowerpot. When the entire rim is covered, cut two long pieces of lace to go around the top and bottom of the rim. Glue them in place.

3 To decorate the bottom of the flowerpot, cut different lengths of lace to make swirls, dots, and short lines. Glue them on the pot and hold them for a minute or two to make sure the design stays where you want it. Let the glue dry.

GOOD IDEA
Use colorful paper strips instead of leather to add designs to a flowerpot.

pogo stick star

Hop to it—these pogo sticks will make you jump for joy!

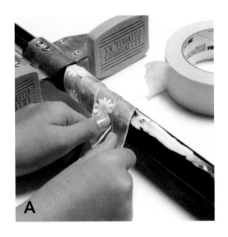

A

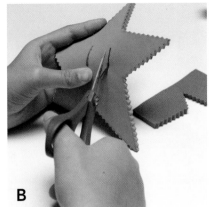

B

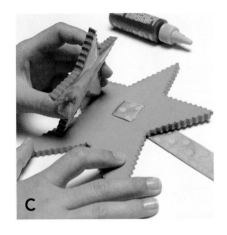

C

YOU'LL NEED

Scissors
2 yards each of two
   colors of ribbon
Pogo stick
Masking tape
Thick white crafts glue
Pencil
Tracing paper
Crafting foam in two
   colors
Pinking shears
   (zigzag scissors)

GOOD IDEA

For a heart design
to trim your pogo
stick, you'll find
patterns on
page 297!

HERE'S HOW

1 Cut a 50-inch-long piece from each color of ribbon.

2 With two of the ribbon ends even and side by side, tape the ribbons to one end of the pogo stick. Spread a line of glue a few inches long just below the tape.

3 Begin winding the ribbon around the stick to cover the tape and glue as shown in Photo A, *above*. Keep winding the ribbon around the stick, adding more glue as you wrap.

4 Trim any extra ribbon at the other end and tie a bow around the top. Trim the ribbon tails the same length.

5 Trace the patterns, on *page 296 or 297*, onto tracing paper. Cut out the patterns and trace around them onto the crafting foam.

6 Cut out the shapes with pinking shears or straight-edge scissors. Bend the large star and cut two 1-inch slits in the center (see Photo B).

7 Pull the remaining piece of ribbon through the slits of the foam shape. Spread glue over the back of the small star and glue it on the large star, covering the slits and the ribbon (see Photo C). Tie the star to the pogo stick. Trim the ribbon ends if necessary.

continued on page 296

pogo stick star

Trace these patterns
to add stars
to your pogo stick!

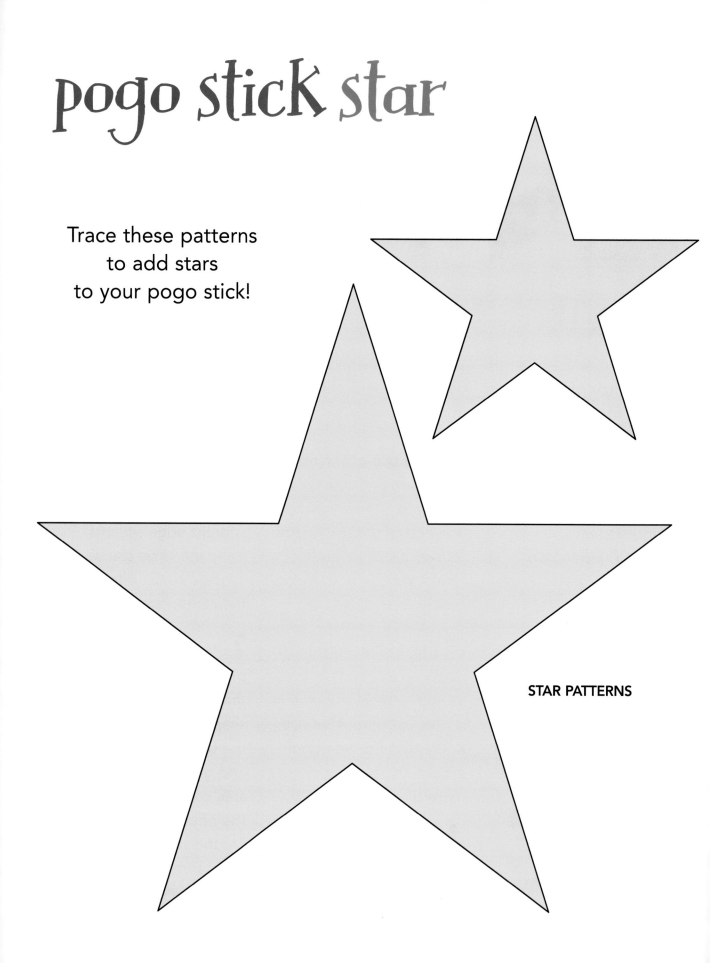

STAR PATTERNS

Trace these patterns
to add hearts
to your pogo stick!

HEART PATTERNS

cuddle-up mittens

Your hands will stay toasty warm in these mittens and gloves that are so playful you'll want to wear them all day!

YOU'LL NEED

Scissors
Cardboard
Gloves or mittens
Needle
Embroidery floss
Thread to match gloves
  or mittens
Beads, buttons, and
  sequins
Fur trim

HERE'S HOW

1 Cut cardboard to fit into the palm of the glove or mitten. Slip it inside to keep you from sewing your glove together. Thread your needle with a thread to match your gloves (ask a grown-up to help if you need it). Use a double strand about 12 inches long. Knot the end.

2 Insert the needle where you want to attach a bead, button, or sequin. Catch the surface of the glove and sew a small stitch as shown in

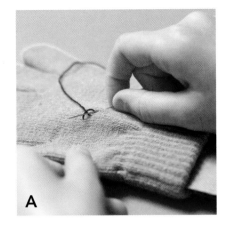

A

B

Photo A. Go over that same stitch two or three times so that it will hold. Trim the extra thread beyond the knot.

3 String the bead onto the needle and insert the needle back into the glove. After the bead is sewed on, sew two or three more stitches in the glove to make sure it stays on. You can layer sequins and beads for a fun look as shown in Photo B.

4 To sew a line, such as a mouth, use three strands of black embroidery floss and sew stitches close together. Sew fur around the cuff if you like.

Sources

Beads are available at most art, crafts, stitchery, and discount stores.
FOR MORE INFORMATION, contact Wichelt Imports, Inc. at Stoddard, WI 54658 or at www.wichelt.com or www.millhill.com.
ALSO CONTACT Westrim Crafts at 7855 Hayvenhurst Ave., Van Nuys, CA 91406 or at www.westrimcrafts.com or call 800/727-2727.
ANOTHER BEAD SOURCE is Bodacious Beads, 1942 River Rd., Des Plaines, IL 60018 or call 847/699-7959.

Buttons are available at most fabric, crafts, stitchery, and discount stores.
FOR MORE INFORMATION, contact JHB International at www.sales@buttons.com or call 303-751-8100.

Clay is available at most art, crafts, and discount stores.
FOR MORE INFORMATION ON SCULPEY III CLAY, contact Polyform Products Co. at 1901 Estes Ave., Elk Grove Village, IL 60007 or at www.sculpey.com.
FOR INFORMATION ON CRAYOLA MODEL MAGIC, contact www.crayola.com or call 800/CRAYOLA.

Decorative-Edge Scissors are available at most art and crafts stores.
FOR MORE INFORMATION, contact Fiskars Brands, Inc. at 305 S. 84th Ave., Wausau, WI 54401 or at www.fiskars.com or call 715/842-2091.

Decorative Papers are available at most art stores.
FOR MORE INFORMATION, contact www.shoptheartstore.com.

Decoupage Medium is available at most art, crafts, and discount stores.
FOR MORE INFORMATION, contact Plaid Enterprises at P.O. Box 2835, Norcross, GA 30091 or call 800/842-4197.

Embroidery Floss is available at most stitchery, discount, and crafts stores.
FOR MORE INFORMATION, contact Anchor Consumer Service Department at P.O. Box 27067, Greenville, SC 29616.
ALSO CONTACT DMC at Port Kearney Bldg. 10, South Kearney, NJ 07032-0650 or at www.dmc-usa.com.
ALSO CONTACT Herrschners at www.herrschners.com or call 800/441-0838.

Leather Lacing is available at most art and crafts stores.
FOR MORE INFORMATION, contact www.michaels.com or call 800/michaels.

Paint is available at most art and crafts stores.
FOR MORE INFORMATION, contact Plaid Enterprises at P.O. Box 2835, Norcross, GA 30091 or at www.plaidonline.com or call 800/842-4197.
ALSO CONTACT DecoArt Paint at P.O. Box 386, Stanford, KY 40484 or call 800/367-3047.

FOR MORE INFORMATION ON GLASS PAINT, contact Delta Technical Coatings, Inc. at 2550 Pellissier Place, Whittier, CA 90601-1505 or at www.deltacrafts.com or call 800/423-4135.
ALSO CONTACT Liquitex Glossies at Binney & Smith, Inc., 1100 Church Lane, Easton, PA 18044-0431.

Ribbon is available at fabric and crafts stores.
FOR MORE INFORMATION, contact Berwick Offray at 2015 W. Front St., Berwick, PA 18603 or at www.berwickindustries.com or call 800/237-9425.

Thick White Crafts Glue is available at most art, crafts, and discount stores.
FOR MORE INFORMATION, contact Aleene's Tacky Glue at www.duncancrafts.com.

Wire is available at most art and crafts stores.
FOR MORE INFORMATION ON METALLIC WIRE, contact Artistic Wire, Ltd., at 752 N. Larch Ave., Elmhurst, IL 60126 or at www.artisticwire.com or call 630/530-7567.
FOR MORE INFORMATION ON PLASTIC-COATED COLORED WIRE, contact Twisteez at www.twisteez.com.

glossary

Acrylic Paint—water-based, quick-drying paint that cleans up with soap and water. Some are developed for outdoor use while others are for interior use only.

Base Coat—a first coat of paint that is used to prepare a surface for more paint or to provide a background color.

Bleed—in crafting terms, when colors run together, usually referring to paint.

Chenille Stem—a velvety covered wire (pipe cleaner) that can be purchased in a variety of sizes and colors, including metallic. Some pipe cleaners are striped.

Collage—combined pieces of paper glued on a surface.

Decorative-edge Scissors—scissors that cut paper scallops, zigzags, waves, and other decorative designs.

Decoupage—the technique of cutting out designs (usually from paper) and mounting them on a surface using decoupage medium or a half-and-half mixture of glue and water.

Decoupage Medium—a gluelike substance that holds paper or other materials in place and leaves a dull or shiny coat.

Disposable—something meant to be used once and then thrown away.

Dowel—a solid cylinder of wood that comes in many sizes.

Embroidery Floss—colored skeins of thread usually used for cross-stitch and other types of needlework.

Enamel Paint—a glossy, colored, opaque paint used to decorate a variety of surfaces. Enamel paint can be water- or oil-based.

Felt—a fabric usually made of wool or cotton that does not fray.

Fringe—a border or trim of cords or threads, hanging loose or tied in bunches.

Gems—in crafting terms, a plastic rhinestone or smooth colorful stone that is backed with metallic silver to make it sparkle.

Glossy—having a smooth, shiny appearance or finish.

Grommet—a metal eyelet that secures to fabric or paper.

Iridescent—showing changes in color when seen from different angles.

Knead—to mix by pressing and squeezing materials, such as clay, together.

Overlap—to have the edges of two or more things layered one on top of the other.

Photocopier—a machine that reproduces an image at full size, reduced, or enlarged, in black and white or color.

Pipe Cleaner—see "Chenille Stem" *above left*.

Pony Beads—colorful plastic beads (round and shapes), ranging from about the size of a pea to the size of a nickel, with a large hole in the center of each.

Shank—the tiny metal loop on the back of some buttons.

Technique—the method used to do artwork, such as painting, cross-stitching, or decoupaging.

Texture—the appearance or feel of a surface.

Thick White Crafts Glue—a bottled glue that is white and thick yet dries clear.

Tracing—drawing around an object or copying the lines of drawn art.

Tracing Paper—a thin sheet of semi-transparent paper used to trace drawings or patterns.

Varnish—a final finish, satin, semi-gloss, or gloss that protects a surface.

Watercolor—a type of paint (available in tubes or as hard cakes) that mixes with water before application. When wet colors are applied side by side they bleed together.

Waxed Paper—available in rolls, this paper has a moisture-proof coating and is often used to cover a work surface when crafting.

Wiggle Eyes—available in a variety of colors, these plastic eyes have flat backs for gluing or shanks for sewing.

301

index

continued on page 304

index